Overcoming Your Eating Disorder

EDITOR-IN-CHIEF

David H. Barlow, PhD

SCIENTIFIC
ADVISORY BOARD

Anne Marie Albano, PhD

Jack M. Gorman, MD

Peter E. Nathan, PhD

Paul Salkovskis, PhD

Bonnie Spring, PhD

John R. Weisz, PhD

G. Terence Wilson, PhD

Overcoming Your Eating Disorder

A Cognitive-Behavioral Therapy Approach for Bulimia Nervosa and Binge-Eating Disorder

Guided Self-Help Workbook

W. Stewart Agras • Robin F. Apple

UNIVERSITY PRESS

2008

OXFORD
UNIVERSITY PRESS

Oxford University Press, Inc., publishes works that further
Oxford University's objective of excellence
in research, scholarship, and education.

Oxford   New York
Auckland   Cape Town   Dar es Salaam   Hong Kong   Karachi
Kuala Lumpur   Madrid   Melbourne   Mexico City   Nairobi
New Delhi   Shanghai   Taipei   Toronto

With offices in
Argentina   Austria   Brazil   Chile   Czech Republic   France   Greece
Guatemala   Hungary   Italy   Japan   Poland   Portugal   Singapore
South Korea   Switzerland   Thailand   Turkey   Ukraine   Vietnam

Copyright © 2008 by Oxford University Press, Inc.

Published by Oxford University Press, Inc.
198 Madison Avenue, New York, New York 10016

www.oup.com

Oxford is a registered trademark of Oxford University Press

All rights reserved. No part of this publication may be reproduced,
stored in a retrieval system, or transmitted, in any form or by any means,
electronic, mechanical, photocopying, recording, or otherwise,
without the prior permission of Oxford University Press.

ISBN 978-0-19-533456-2

About Treatments*ThatWork*™

One of the most difficult problems confronting patients with various disorders and diseases is finding the best help available. Everyone knows friends or family who have sought treatment from a seemingly reputable practitioner only to find out later from another doctor that the original diagnosis was wrong or the treatments recommended were inappropriate or perhaps even harmful. Most patients, or their family members, address this problem by reading everything they can about their symptoms, seeking information on the Internet, or aggressively "asking around" to tap knowledge from friends and acquaintances. Governments and healthcare policymakers are also aware that people in need don't always get the best treatments—something they refer to as "variability in healthcare practices."

Now healthcare systems around the world are attempting to correct this variability by introducing "evidence-based practice." This simply means that it is in everyone's interest that patients get the most up-to-date and effective care for a particular problem. Healthcare policymakers have also recognized that it is very useful to give consumers of healthcare as much information as possible so that they can make intelligent decisions in a collaborative effort to improve health and mental health. This series, Treatments*ThatWork*™, is designed to accomplish just that. Only the latest and most effective interventions for particular problems are described, in user-friendly language. To be included in this series, each treatment program must pass the highest standards of evidence available, as determined by a scientific advisory board. Thus, when individuals suffering from these problems, or their family members, seek out an expert clinician who is familiar with these interventions and decides that they are appropriate, they will have confidence that they are receiving the best care available. Of course, only your healthcare professional can decide on the right mix of treatments for you.

Cognitive-behavioral therapy (CBT) has been proven effective for treating bulimia nervosa and binge-eating disorder. However, this type of program requires at least 6 months of weekly sessions with a qualified mental health professional. If you suffer from an eating disorder and want to get treatment but have little time to devote to therapy, a shorter, time-limited program may be right for you.

This workbook outlines a guided self-help (GSH) program based on the principles of CBT. Although sessions with a therapist or clinician are required, there are usually no more than 12, and each one is only 25 minutes long. You will do much of the treatment on your own, using the workbook as your guide. You will learn and practice the skills you need to overcome your eating disorder and establish healthy habits, while consulting with your therapist for encouragement and support. Through monitoring your eating patterns daily, and employing strategies such as challenging negative thoughts and using formal problem solving, you will reduce your desire to binge and purge. GSH is hard work, but the benefits are well worth it. If you have the desire and the drive, you can use this workbook to eliminate your eating disorder once and for all.

David H. Barlow, Editor-in-Chief
Treatments *ThatWork*™
Boston, Massachusetts

Contents

Information About Bulimia Nervosa, Binge-Eating Disorder, and This Treatment Program

Chapter 1   Introduction   *3*

Chapter 2   Binge Eating and Purging   *5*

Chapter 3   Health Effects of Binge Eating and Purging   *13*

Chapter 4   Treatments for Binge Eating and Purging   *23*

Chapter 5   Evidence for the Effectiveness of Guided Self-Help   *31*

A Step-by-Step Approach to Treatment

Chapter 6   An Assessment of Your Eating Problems: Is It Time to Begin Treatment?   *35*

Chapter 7   Understanding and Applying the CBT Model   *41*

Chapter 8   Using Daily Food Records to Monitor Eating   *45*

Chapter 9   Establishing a Regular Pattern of Eating Plus Weekly Weighing   *53*

Chapter 10   Feared and Problem Foods   *59*

Chapter 11   Body-Image Concerns   *67*

Chapter 12   Handling Intense Moods and Emotions   *71*

Chapter 13   Working Through Problem Situations and Thoughts   *77*

Chapter 14   Handling Challenging People   *87*

Chapter 15   Preventing Relapse and Maintaining Change   *91*

About the Authors   *99*

Information About Bulimia Nervosa, Binge-Eating Disorder, and This Treatment Program

Chapter 1 — *Introduction*

This book describes therapist-assisted self-help, more commonly known as guided self-help (GSH). It is for individuals who suffer from binge eating with or without purging, disorders known as bulimia nervosa (BN) and binge-eating disorder (BED). It should be used with the help of a therapist or other qualified mental health professional. It is not meant as a stand-alone self-help book. Although the book provides the bulk of the material to be addressed in therapy, you also need to attend 25-minute sessions with a clinician who provides advice and helps keep you on track. You can expect the therapist to often refer you back to the book when you have questions. In other words, you are in charge of your treatment. In addition, this treatment is time-limited, meaning there are fewer, shorter sessions than in the full cognitive-behavioral treatment program that this workbook is based on. You make up for this by using the book as "take-home therapy" to be used between sessions. Usually there are about 8–12 treatment sessions. Of course, a shorter treatment does not appeal to everyone, and some may choose to have the more intensive treatment, which typically consists of 6 full months of weekly, 50-minute sessions. If you are interested in the full treatment, please consult *Overcoming Your Eating Disorder: A Cognitive-Behavioral Therapy Approach for Bulimia Nervosa and Binge-Eating Disorder, Workbook, Second Edition* (Oxford).

The first part of this workbook briefly describes what we know about bulimia nervosa and binge-eating disorder, how these disorders affect health and well-being, and the evidence for the effectiveness of the cognitive-behavioral therapy (CBT) program on which this book in based. In addition, the growing evidence for the effectiveness of therapist-assisted self-help is described. For many people, therapist-assisted self-help may be as effective as full-scale CBT.

The second part of the book describes the therapy, which is divided into several steps. These steps have been carefully sequenced and build on each other. Each step should be followed in the order it appears. It is particularly important to master each step before moving on. You and your therapist together will decide when it is time to move to the next step.

Therapy begins with a 50-minute session so that your therapist can learn about your eating disorder and get to know you. After this initial session, you will meet with your therapist once a week over the next 3 to 4 weeks for approximately 25 minutes each time. Although these meetings are important, what you do and the changes you make in between sessions are what really count. Make no mistake about it, it is no easy task to overcome binge eating or binge eating and purging. You have to be ready to change. After the first 4 weeks, sessions are spaced every 2 weeks, and after a couple of months, they are spaced at monthly intervals. The reason to space the sessions as treatment goes along is to give you more time to work on your problem eating on your own. Usually there are about 10 sessions, but both the number of sessions and their spacing may vary, depending on your therapist's view of your progress.

Chapter 2 — *Binge Eating and Purging*

Bulimia nervosa involves frequent episodes of binge eating, almost always followed by purging and intense feelings of guilt or shame. Purging is a way for bulimics to exert control over their weight or shape. Body concerns unduly influence individuals' perception of themselves. Although the formal diagnostic criteria require that binge eating and purging occur at least twice a week over a period of 3 months, those who engage in these behaviors less frequently may also need treatment.

There are two forms of bulimia. The first is characterized by binge eating and some form of purging. The second is called non-purging bulimia nervosa and consists of episodes of fasting or excessive exercise without purging.

Binge-eating disorder (BED) is different from bulimia nervosa in that binge eaters don't usually purge and they are often overweight or obese. Also, to obtain a diagnosis of BED, a person must have engaged in the behavior for longer than 3 months. As with bulimia nervosa, those who binge less frequently may also need treatment.

Some form of binge eating and purging affects about 5% of women in the United States, and a similar percentage of women in most Western countries. The disorder also appears to be spreading into less developed countries. Men appear to be less susceptible to bulimia nervosa, with about 1 man affected for every 10 women with the disorder. However, binge-eating disorder occurs more frequently in men than bulimia nervosa, with about two men affected for every three women with the disorder. Both binge-eating disorder and bulimia nervosa begin during adolescence or early adulthood. However, many of the associated behaviors, such as excessively dieting and using other methods to control weight, being preoccupied with body shape, and occasionally binge eating or purging begin earlier, sometimes in early childhood. Binge-eating disorder is often, but not always, associated with overweight and obesity. Studies have shown that as weight increases, the proportion of individuals with binge eating also increases.

A recent family study suggested that binge eating and obesity are distinct from one another and that binge-eating disorder separately increased the risk for overweight, particularly severe overweight. In this study, 300 individuals with and without binge-eating disorder, and more than 1,500 of their family members, were interviewed. For those with a diagnosis of binge-eating disorder, 20% of their family members also had binge-eating disorder. For those individuals not diagnosed with binge-eating disorder, just less than 10% of of their family members had the disorder. Hence, binge-eating disorder clearly runs in families.

Some studies suggest that bulimia nervosa tends to run in families as well. Twin studies suggest that bulimia nervosa is genetic and inheritable, although the exact nature of what is inherited remains unknown. Other studies suggest that individuals with bulimia may have lower levels of serotonin than people without the disorder and that bingeing on high-carbohydrate foods tends to alleviate the condition. Serotonin is a chemical in the brain that regulates mood, emotion, sleep, and appetite. Low serotonin levels may also be associated with depression, which frequently accompanies bulimia.

Environmental factors may also lead to bulimia and binge eating. The pressure on women to be thin has increased in the last 25 years. This appears to be due to a portrayal of ever-thinner ideal body types in the media combined with a rise in popularity of various types of commercial diet programs. Other factors that may contribute to eating disorders include having a family history of obesity, being teased about weight and shape by peers during adolescence, and having low self-esteem.

Low self-esteem combined with weight and shape concerns form the basis for the further development of bulimia nervosa and binge-eating disorder. Concern with weight and shape eventually gives rise to attempts to control weight and shape by dieting. Often, such dieting is successful in inducing weight loss but is eventually followed by loss of control over eating, leading to binge eating.

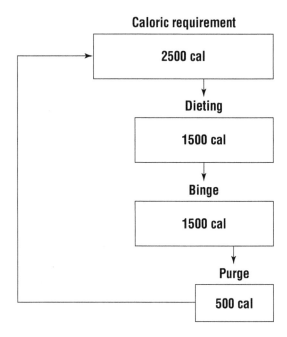

Figure 2.1 An Example of Caloric Balance in Bulimia Nervosa

A simple way to view this is to consider a binge as the body's way of defeating dieting and maintaining the necessary caloric balance, in which energy intake and expenditure are equal. Figure 2.1 shows an example of how the body balances caloric intake and expenditure. If a person requires 2,500 calories per day and restricts herself to only 1,500, she is creating a deficit of 1,000 calories. If she binges to make up for this deficit, she will likely eat too much, consuming around 1,500 calories. To eliminate the additional 500 calories, she then purges. So, if you restrict your food intake for too long, your body will take over and basically "force" you to binge to make up for the caloric deficit you created by dieting. Moreover, because your body is in a hurry to obtain adequate nutrition, you will find yourself craving easily swallowed and quickly absorbed foods that are high in fat and sugar. As you can see, this is the start of a vicious cycle of dieting, followed by binge eating, followed by more dieting, and so on. Purging, which can be viewed as another form of dieting, simply makes the situation worse, leading to larger binges. Those with BED consume an average of around 1,000 calories in a binge. Bulimics tend to consume 1,500 calories or more during a binge episode.

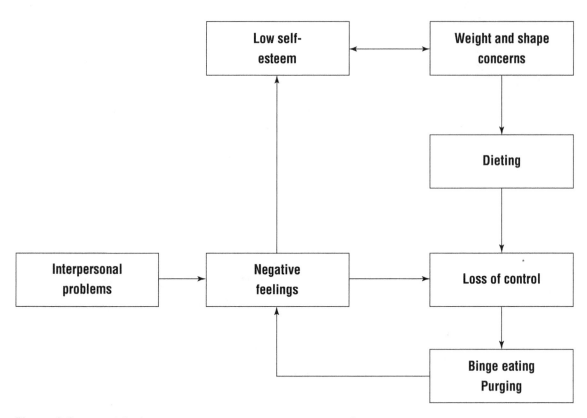

Figure 2.2 A Model of Factors Maintaining Binge Eating and Purging

As can be seen in Figure 2.2, an even broader vicious circle results. Although binge eating and purging may lead to a temporary feeling of relief, they also quickly lead to self-blame, with feelings of guilt and depression. These negative feelings lower self-esteem even further, aggravating weight and shape concerns and causing the whole cycle to begin again. Negative feelings also result from faulty interpersonal relationships, whether the interactions are with friends, a boss, or a spouse. These feelings can likewise lead to a loss of control over eating, particularly when individuals are hungry because they have been dieting. In a hungry state, we have less control over our feelings and our behavior.

Some individuals have difficulty dealing with negative feelings or intense emotions of any type. Instead of handling the situation that caused these feelings, these individuals try to avoid the feelings altogether by binge eating.

Breaking the cycle of binge eating and purging is extremely difficult. The key to regaining control over your eating is to overcome dieting.

This can be accomplished first by eating meals and snacks at regular intervals, not more than 4 to 5 hours apart. Once eating patterns have been normalized, the next step is to stop restricting your diet. One way to do this is by gradually incorporating foods you fear and avoid into your diet. This forms the first step and is the basis for all other steps in this treatment program. There is good evidence supporting the effectiveness of this first step. In a study done at Stanford University, individuals with bulimia nervosa were treated with cognitive-behavioral therapy. Of those who came closest to increasing their regularity of eating by consuming three meals and two snacks each day, 70% were no longer binge eating and purging at the end of treatment. On the other hand, of those who hardly changed their eating patterns, only 5% were no longer binge eating or purging at the end of treatment. These dramatic differences in outcome attest to the importance of this first step in treatment.

Binge Eating

Binge eating is the consumption of large amounts of food in a relatively short time accompanied by a feeling of loss of control over eating. Most individuals engaged in a binge will stop eating only when they are interrupted or when they feel uncomfortably full from having eaten too much. Binges can be large or small. It is important to distinguish between the two types of binges because during treatment large binges tend to disappear first, smaller ones later.

The foods consumed in small, or subjective, binges are usually characterized as "forbidden" by the individual and commonly include such items as chocolate, ice cream, or pastries.

The foods consumed in large, or objective, binges are usually sweet and high in fat content. Such foods may include ice cream, milk shakes, bread with butter and jam, cakes, cookies, cereals, pasta, and so on. Large binges do not tend to consist of meals (e.g., meat and potatoes). Some examples of binges follow.

Binge 1: An entire large pizza, 20 breadsticks, four large slices of cake

Binge 2: Two big plates of pasta with broccoli, zucchini, and tomato sauce; half an avocado with a large plate of salad greens; three bowls of nonfat chocolate and vanilla ice cream

Binge 3: Five to six bowls of oats with brown sugar and strawberries, a plate of couscous, beans, broccoli, and peas left over from lunch, a heaped-up plate of oats with honey and ice cream.

As can be seen, there is much variety in binges, although each person may have favorite binge foods. There is, however, another type of binge eating, known as grazing, where individuals eat small amounts of snack foods every few minutes throughout the day. In the end, these small amounts add up to a considerable amount of food.

We have seen some of the triggers for binge eating, namely, dieting, hunger, and negative emotions. Other triggers that can contribute to binge eating when combined with hunger and negative feelings may include having a small piece of a "forbidden" food, drinking alcohol, having a fight with someone close to you, reading a magazine with feature articles on staying in shape, and so on. These triggers, combined with eating very little earlier in the day and with chronically dieting, will likely lead to a rather large binge.

The immediate triggers for a binge can be quite complex, although all of them are potentially remediable. Although binges may be caused by triggers, they also, in a sense, serve to trigger a number of consequences, including numbing the emotions or even obliterating the triggering concerns.

Purging

Self-Induced Vomiting

Not everyone who binges also purges. Those with binge-eating disorder do not purge while suffering from this disorder, although some may have done so in the past. As discussed earlier however, bulimia nervosa is characterized by binge eating followed by purging. The most common method of purging is self-induced vomiting. To facilitate vomiting, many individuals consume large amounts of fluids with their binges. Usually, putting a finger or other object down the throat facilitates purging. After some time, purging may become automatic.

Another way of inducing vomiting is to use ipecac. This syrupy medication causes nausea and vomiting within about 20 minutes of ingestion. It is intended to be used in emergencies and should be administered only if someone has swallowed poison. Ipecac is particularly dangerous because it causes systemic toxicity, which can cause weakness, tenderness and stiffness of muscles, cardiac disease and heart failure, coma, seizures, shock, blood pressure increases, possible hemorrhage, dehydration, aspiration pneumonia, and death.

Self-induced vomiting is not an effective way to rid the body of calories. One study conducted in a clinical research center examined the number of calories eaten and the number of calories purged in patients with bulimia nervosa. Regardless of the size of their binges, patients retained approximately 1,000 calories after purging. This is equivalent to one or two meals and shows that the body is making up for having missed adequate meals earlier in the day. If the body did not retain these calories, bulimics would continue to lose weight. However, the vast majority of bulimics maintain a stable weight or even gain weight despite regularly purging.

Laxatives

The next most common form of purging is the use of stimulant laxatives. These work by stimulating the muscles of the lower bowel. When taken regularly and in large doses, laxatives cause the bowel muscles to stop working by themselves, leading to constipation. The use of laxatives is an even more inefficient way of removing calories from the body. Studies have found that, at most, about 10% of calories are removed, even with excessive laxative use. Moreover, as we have seen, removing calories simply leads to larger binges.

Diuretics

The third most common form of purging involves taking diuretics or water pills. Many bulimics use water pills because they give the illusion of a flatter stomach. One may feel better because of fluid loss, but water pills do nothing to remove calories from the body.

All forms of purging are inefficient methods of controlling caloric intake; in other words, they do not work.

Over-Exercising

Another method many bulimics use to control caloric intake is to increase energy expenditure through exercise. As mentioned earlier, there is a non-purging form of bulimia nervosa associated with excessive exercise or fasting, in which individuals do not consume solid foods and subsist only on fluids such as water, coffee, or tea for longer than 24 hours at a time and often up to several days. Such fasting is then followed by a return to binge eating. Many bulimics purge and exercise. In the case of exercise, we are not talking about exercise to improve health. Many individuals with an eating disorder engage in vigorous exercise for two or more hours every day. Such exercise often takes over their lives so that it must be performed even if they are injured or unwell, or if it interferes with their social life. After this sort of strenuous exercise, individuals are often exhausted, but they persist day after day. Sometimes it seems to them that exercise is their only pleasure in life.

This chapter has introduced a model of factors underlying the maintenance of binge eating, and also factors that cause binge eating, such as heredity and environmental triggers. We have also examined binge eating in some detail, including the immediate triggers of binge eating. Finally, we considered various forms of purging. In the next chapter, we will take a look at some of the health effects of binge eating and purging.

Chapter 3 *Health Effects of Binge Eating and Purging*

Binge eating and purging and accompanying behaviors, such as dieting and excessive physical exercise, can be harmful to your health. Common complications of these behaviors can affect your heart, brain function, bones, teeth, and digestive system. In general, severe dieting associated with low weight will also be associated with cardiovascular problems, menstrual problems, and osteoporosis (a disease characterized by low bone mass and the structural deterioration of bone tissue). Overweight, seen mostly with binge-eating disorder, is associated with all the problems of overweight and obesity, including diabetes, high cholesterol levels, and high blood pressure.

Dieting

Reducing the number of calories you consume also cuts your intake of necessary minerals, such as calcium, potassium, and magnesium, in addition to vitamins, although outright vitamin deficiency is rarely seen in bulimia nervosa or binge-eating disorder. Fluid intake may also be reduced, leading to dehydration. As well, because bulimics tend to avoid what they perceive as fattening foods, they may cut protein and fat intake. Some of these deficiencies are corrected by the amount and type of food eaten during binges, creating a mixed picture, depending on the severity of dietary restriction and binge eating. Nonetheless, low-weight individuals may experience low blood pressure and heart rate as a result of strict dieting, giving rise to feelings of weakness and dizziness, and sometimes fainting. These feelings may be aggravated by the dehydration that accompanies food restriction, which is of course worsened by purging methods such as vomiting, using laxatives and diuretics, and exercising excessively. Calcium and protein deficiencies may lead to a reduction of bone density (osteopenia) and ultimately to osteoporosis. When osteopenia or osteoporosis is combined with excessive exercise, the risk of stress fractures is much increased. Occasionally, anemia (a reduction in red blood cells and/or hemoglobin) may occur as a complication of dieting.

Because of the caloric and fluid restriction associated with dieting, thinking may become difficult and disorganized. In simple terms, one is not ingesting enough energy to fuel the normal functioning of the brain. Difficulties in thinking may affect work performance and interpersonal relationships. In addition, many bulimics find themselves continually thinking about dieting and binge eating. Such obsessive thoughts act as a distraction and may also interfere with work and other activities.

Both skin and hair may also suffer. Dieting and the resultant lack of protein may lead to increasingly brittle hair and eventually, when combined with a drop in weight, to hair loss. Skin may also become drier and may be more susceptible to infection. Losing too much weight may also lead to irregular menstruation or to amenorrhea (the absence of menstruation), and excessive exercise may exacerbate these problems.

Purging

Because purging, particularly in the form of self-induced vomiting, results in a loss of calories and causes dehydration, it makes the deficiencies associated with dieting only that much worse. In addition, electrolytes such as potassium may be lost. About 5% of purging bulimics have significantly lowered levels of potassium, one of the most dangerous complications of bulimia, and one that should be immediately corrected with potassium supplements taken under the direction of a physician who can frequently monitor potassium levels. Potassium loss can be dangerous because it alters the action of the heart, causing arrhythmias (abnormal heart rhythms), which can occasionally lead to sudden death in low-weight bulimic individuals. Because of the force used to bring up food, self-induced vomiting can tear the esophagus, which may result in one's spitting up blood.

One sign associated with purging, particularly self-induced vomiting, is swelling of the parotid glands, which are behind the ears and below the jaw. The swelling is often painful, similar to that experienced with mumps.

Dental problems are one of the most frequent complications of purging. Indeed, most individuals who have purged regularly for 4 or more years have dental complications. Acid in the mouth from self-induced vomiting leads to erosion of tooth enamel, sometimes to the point where fillings rise above the surface of the tooth that has been eroded away. Binge eating sweet foods probably makes this problem worse and contributes to tooth decay. It is not unusual for these problems to lead to gum disease and dental abscesses, with tooth loss and sometimes bone loss. Bulimics often brush their teeth immediately after purging. This, however, causes further enamel erosion because the acid softens the enamel. After purging, it is better to rinse the mouth with a teaspoon of baking soda dissolved in water, an alkaline solution that neutralizes acid.

Over-Exercising

Excessive exercise may be associated with menstrual disturbances, including amenorrhea (loss of the menstrual cycle), that may become chronic. Such exercise is associated with lower estrogen levels that, in turn, may worsen osteoporosis. Excessive exercise is also associated with a variety of sports injuries, including stress fractures, which are aggravated by dieting and osteoporosis. In addition, exercising vigorously in hot weather increases dehydration and may aggravate potassium loss, causing an irregular heartbeat and sometimes death. Clearly, one must use common sense when exercising, and all exercise should be done in moderation. One should feel relaxed after exercise, not tired or exhausted.

Laxatives and Diuretics

The use of large doses of over-the-counter stimulant laxatives can lead to constipation and dehydration and may increase potassium loss. In addition, laxatives may cause melanosis coli, a condition in which the lining of the large intestine turns dark brown or black. This is a harmless condition and will reverse when laxative use is discontinued. The use of diuretics or water pills also causes dehydration and leads to potassium loss. Prolonged use can lead to kidney damage and occasionally to kidney failure, requiring dialysis.

Bulimia Nervosa and Diabetes

Medical research has found that type 1 diabetes, with onset typically occurring in childhood or adolescence, is more common in bulimics than in those who do not have the disorder. In type 1 diabetes, the body's immune system destroys the cells in the pancreas that make insulin. It is sometimes called insulin-dependent diabetes because it requires treatment with insulin. Unfortunately, some of the behaviors associated with bulimia can worsen the medical complications of diabetes. For example, binge eating and purging make controlling diabetes much more difficult. Some individuals with bulimia stop taking their insulin in order to lose weight, and this worsens the control of their diabetes. Most medical research suggests that bulimics are more likely to have more long-term medical complications than are other patients with type 1 diabetes. The worst combination seems to be withholding insulin combined with binge eating and purging. One study found that 70% of such individuals had some form of nerve damage; half had retinopathy, a condition in which eyesight gradually deteriorates and which may lead to blindness; and a quarter had kidney problems that can ultimately lead to kidney failure. Other complications included high blood pressure and stroke. Given these extra complications, it is critically important for bulimics with diabetes to overcome their binge eating and purging.

Binge Eating

The most obvious consequence of binge eating is weight gain and potential obesity. In addition, binge eating may lead to feelings of bloating, abdominal pain, and nausea. Very rarely, complications such as gastric dilatation or even rupture of the stomach caused by ingesting large amounts of food may occur. The combination of dieting, binge eating, and purging may also slow digestion, which can lead to abdominal pain, bloating, and nausea. As noted earlier, bingeing on sweet foods may aggravate the dental problems frequently seen in bulimia nervosa.

Overweight, Obesity, and Binge Eating

Although some individuals with bulimia nervosa may be overweight, binge-eating disorder is most likely to be associated with overweight and obesity. As the degree of overweight and obesity increases, so does the proportion of those with binge-eating disorder. As noted in Chapter 2, it is now thought that binge-eating disorder and obesity are separate disorders with different causes, although they often run in the same families. Clearly, binge eating will lead to, or aggravate, overweight and obesity. Although stopping binge eating does not lead to weight loss in the short run, studies have shown that, over a longer term, those who stop binge eating are likely to weigh 10–15 lbs less than those who do not stop. Although this may not seem like a lot of weight to lose, the health effects of losing even 10 lbs can be quite significant. One problem for the binge eater is that dieting to lose weight will aggravate binge eating, as shown in Figure 2.2 in Chapter 2. Ultimately, dieting will lead to weight gain rather than weight loss. This is why it may be better to first overcome binge eating and then to gradually develop healthy eating and exercise habits.

Developing a healthy lifestyle, of course, is very difficult to do in today's world. In the United States, about 3,900 calories are produced by the food industry for every person in the country. This is almost double the caloric requirement for the average person. Moreover, it is the job of the food industry to sell all those calories. On top of all this, it is increasingly difficult to exercise enough. There are too few sidewalks in most communities, not all communities are safe to walk around, and almost no one can walk to work anymore. This is why it is so difficult for overweight persons to lose weight. Essentially, one has to defend oneself against an environment that predisposes to overweight and obesity.

A reminder, however: this book is *not* about weight loss. It is aimed at treating eating disorders that contribute their own burdens to poor mental and physical health.

Some of the medical problems associated with overweight and obesity are listed here, and many individuals with binge-eating disorder and overweight or obesity have more than one of these conditions:

- High cholesterol levels or high levels of triglycerides
- High blood pressure
- Type 2 diabetes
- Heart disease and coronary artery disease
- Stroke
- Gallbladder disease
- Osteoarthritis
- Sleep apnea (long pauses between breathing during sleep, followed by snoring)
- Some cancers (endometrial, or uterine; breast; and colon)

All these disorders are potentially treatable, but it is better to try to avoid them in the first place. Stopping binge eating is a good first step in this process. Although the various medical complications associated with binge eating and purging should be taken seriously, the effects on individuals' lives are even more pronounced and often more disabling than the physical complications.

Life Effects of Binge Eating and Purging

There are two ways in which binge eating and purging affect people's lives. First are the direct effects of binge eating and purging. Second are the effects of associated psychological disorders.

Effects of Binge Eating and Purging on Daily Life

We have seen that binge eating and purging can lead directly to various medical complications. But there are also effects on daily living. Binge eating and purging eventually become a way of life. These behaviors consume a lot of time and demand extra effort. Each episode of bingeing may take an hour or more, and it is not unusual for individuals to have several episodes in a day. Preparing for a binge also takes time. One must buy food and sometimes store it for future binges. This takes time out of the day and also means spending a considerable amount of money on the eating disorder rather than on higher priority items. Moreover, many individuals who binge find themselves preoccupied with thinking about whether or not to eat or whether or not to binge, or about their body shape and weight. This preoccupation may be aggravated by the fact that severe dieting makes it difficult to think clearly. These preoccupations waste time and often interfere with other activities, such as work, thus diminishing one's effectiveness. Many patients who are able to stop binge eating and purging are surprised by the amount of time they now have available for other activities, such as spending time with friends or family and engaging in new interests. They find their lives far richer and more satisfying than they did when they were preoccupied with achieving a certain weight and shape, binge eating, and purging.

Binge eating and purging are also inextricably interwoven with upsetting feelings. As we have seen, instead of dealing directly with events that provoke anger, anxiety, or sadness, binge eaters tend to avoid the whole situation and drown their feelings in food. While this affords temporary relief, the guilt and anxiety about binge eating soon take over, then the binge eater makes some form of resolution to do better tomorrow. Of course, this simply sets the individual up to fail again and to suffer more guilt and anxiety.

Finally, there is the effect on close relationships. Binge eating and purging is often hidden from friends and close companions, introducing deception into the relationship—not a particularly healthy thing to do. In addition, the time and effort spent on binge eating cannot be spent furthering close relationships. This sort of neglect is likely to affect the quality of those relationships. Another problem the disorder creates is difficulty eating with other people. In social situations, one may have to make excuses for not eating very much or not eating foods that other people are enjoying. Eating out and eating with friends may be avoided, which deprives one of a pleasurable aspect of life.

Associated Psychological Disorders

Many individuals with bulimia nervosa or binge-eating disorder have other psychological disorders, too, such as depression, anxiety disorders, or personality problems. Approximately 60% of persons with an eating disorder have experienced depression at some time in their lives. This is far higher than would be expected in the normal population. Additionally, about a quarter of bulimics are suffering from depression at the time they seek treatment. Depression may complicate treatment by reducing the amount of energy people can apply to getting better. Therapists will therefore often recommend that depression be treated before one begins work on the eating disorder. Depression may last from a few weeks to months or, in some cases, many years and may stem from several factors. Poor nutrition caused by excessive dieting, binge eating, and purging, together with weight loss may well cause depression. Extremely excessive exercise can compound depression. In addition, simply having a disorder in which an important part of one's life, namely eating, is out of control may also lead to depression. For some people, being out of control with eating may spread to other areas, such as feeling out of control at work or in personal relationships. In addition, bulimia's harmful effect on close relationships is also likely to lead to depression. Although most people with depression find that their appetite is lessened, those with eating disorders often find that their binge eating gets worse when they are depressed. Depression also adds to difficulty thinking and, of course, will affect work and close relationships because one lacks energy.

Anxiety disorders such as generalized anxiety disorder, panic disorder, and obsessive-compulsive disorder (OCD) are also common in bulimics. Generalized anxiety is characterized by pervasive feelings of anxiousness and excessive worry. In panic disorder, one experiences acute episodes of anxiety characterized by rapid heartbeat, marked anxiety, fears of losing control, and feelings of unreality. These panic attacks may last from a few minutes to an hour, and during them individuals may feel that they are going to die, go insane, or totally lose control and faint. With OCD, one may have unwanted thoughts accompanied by anxiety and may use rituals to help prevent a feared event from occurring. For example, individuals may think that they picked up an infection and then feel compelled to wash their hands over and over again. As with depression, your therapist may suggest treating the anxiety disorder before the eating disorder.

Finally, personality disorders are commonly found in conjunction with an eating disorder. A personality disorder consists of a long-lasting pattern of interpersonal behavior. Such behaviors may complicate any relationship, even a therapeutic relationship, and may get in the way of recovery. In addition, these behaviors or their consequences may trigger binges and may need to be explored in the treatment of bulimia. One characteristic cluster of behaviors includes a history of unstable and intense interpersonal relationships together with impulsivity that is often self-damaging, and may also include difficulty controlling anger. Other behaviors in this cluster may include oversensitivity to the real or imagined loss of a relationship.

Another pattern sees individuals trying to satisfy other people's needs rather than their own, ultimately leading to feelings of anger and feelings of being taken advantage of; as a result, the individual rebels against the relationship. Again, this type of behavior may complicate one's close relationships.

In this chapter, we have covered the various health and life complications of bulimia nervosa and binge-eating disorder. In the next chapter, we will examine the research on treating these two eating disorders.

Chapter 4   *Treatments for Binge Eating and Purging*

Although binge eating and purging have been described for many centuries, it is only relatively recently that bulimia nervosa, and then binge-eating disorder, were well described and accepted as serious medical and psychological disorders. During and after the 1970s there was an upsurge in the number of cases of bulimia nervosa in the clinics of most industrialized countries; this led clinicians and researchers to look for treatments that might work, none being available at that time. Two separate lines of research began almost simultaneously. The first examined the usefulness of antidepressant medication; this was the beginning of pharmacological research concerning eating disorders. The second treatment examined the effectiveness of a psychotherapy known as cognitive-behavioral therapy (CBT), which represents the beginning of psychotherapy research concerning eating disorders. These two lines of research eventually came together to examine the benefits of combining medication and psychotherapy.

Antidepressant Treatment

The early notion that bulimia nervosa was a form of depression led clinicians to use medication to treat the disorder. As we have seen, depression is commonly associated with bulimia nervosa and binge-eating disorder, and that is why some people interpreted bulimia nervosa as a form of depression. However, we now know that the two disorders are quite separate. In fact, researchers have found that, for patients with bulimia and depression, an antidepressant can cure the depression without affecting the bulimia, or vice versa. Nonetheless, researchers at Harvard University conducted a study comparing the effects of antidepressant medication with the effects of a placebo (an inactive medication) on bulimia nervosa. They found that the antidepressant was better than the placebo in reducing binge eating and purging. This finding led to more studies of different antidepressants, with the largest studies eventually using fluoxetine (Prozac). One important finding about fluoxetine was that, in order to be effective in treating bulimia, it had to be given in much higher doses than when used to treat depression. For bulimia nervosa or binge-eating disorder, the effective dose is 60 mg per day as compared to 10–40 mg for depression. Most people find it better to take the medication at night because it has a mild sedative effect. However, some individuals find that Prozac has a slightly stimulant effect. These individuals prefer to take the medication in the morning. In addition, it is important to take medication after the last purging episode of the day so that all or part of the dose will not be purged. Like all medications, Prozac has side effects that some individuals cannot tolerate. In addition to causing drowsiness or having a stimulant effect, Prozac can cause stomach upset, weakness, and hand tremors. It may also cause lowered sexual desire and may interfere with sexual performance.

It turns out that nearly all types of antidepressants are effective for both bulimia nervosa and binge-eating disorder. As we will see, antidepressants are not as effective as CBT, although when combined with CBT they may add to its effectiveness.

Another medication that may hold promise for the treatment of binge-eating disorder is topiramate, a medication used to treat seizures in patients with epilepsy. Although we don't know how this medication works to help control binge eating, some studies suggest that topiramate is more effective in reducing binge eating than is a placebo. It has also been shown to result in an average weight loss of about 10 lbs in overweight individuals. Topiramate causes side effects, including weakness, sudden hunger, difficulty thinking, confusion, mood swings, and depression. At the time this book was written, there had been no studies comparing topiramate with cognitive-behavioral therapy, so the relative effectiveness of the two treatments is unknown.

Psychotherapies

Two psychotherapies have shown promise in the treatment of bulimia nervosa and binge-eating disorder: cognitive-behavioral therapy and interpersonal psychotherapy (IPT). CBT is based on the model of bulimia nervosa described in Chapter 2 (see Figure 2.2) and forms the basis for this self-help workbook. As we look at the model, we can see that therapy can be directed at a number of factors: self-esteem, dieting, interpersonal relationships that lead to negative feelings, and concerns about weight and shape. CBT is aimed at reducing dieting, reinstating a normal pattern of eating, and reducing binge-eating triggers. These aims derive from the clinical estimation that these were the main factors maintaining binge eating and purging. When these factors are changed, binge eating tends to disappear, and in bulimia nervosa purging also disappears, although one may need to pay special attention to laxative and diuretic abuse.

Recent research has shown that reducing dieting is the most important element in decreasing binge eating. Most bulimics tend to either starve themselves early in the day and then lose control of their eating later on or follow an extremely disorganized pattern of eating. Eating this way can make it difficult to recognize true feelings of hunger and fullness, which are key sensations that help us all regulate our eating. The main aim in reducing dieting is to establish a normal eating pattern of three meals and two snacks each day eaten at regular intervals. Reducing the amount of time between eating episodes to no more than 4 hours lessens hunger and diminishes the chance of binge eating.

There is much evidence to suggest the importance of reducing dieting. In one large-scale study, dietary restraint was found to mediate the outcome of cognitive-behavioral therapy. This means that cognitive-behavioral therapy works by reducing dieting. Moreover, a reduction in dieting behavior occurred very early in treatment, within the first two or three sessions. Other studies found reducing purging by 70% or more in the first six sessions of treatment was a powerful indicator of eventual success in treatment, both immediately after treatment had ended and at follow-up 8–12 months later. The likely mechanism for this early predictive effect is that the reduction in dieting leads to reductions in hunger and therefore the likelihood of binge eating is reduced. Once binge eating declines, the need to purge decreases. Finally, as we saw earlier, another study found that 70% of those who were able to come close to a regular pattern of eating (three meals and two snacks each day) were able to stop binge eating and purging by the end of treatment. On the other hand, only about 5% of those who were unable to change their pattern of eating were able to stop binge eating and purging.

One lesson from these findings is that early change in treatment is very important. This means that patients need to make quite rapid changes in their dietary patterns. This involves a degree of psychological risk and anxiety because one may fear gaining weight. It is important to ask yourself if you are ready to make the necessary changes in your behavior and associated attitudes over a period of a few weeks. You must be willing to take a risk in order to get better. Interestingly, the average weight gain in treating bulimia nervosa is essentially zero. However, those who are below their natural weight will gain some weight, and those who are overweight will tend to lose some weight if they stop binge eating.

The effectiveness of cognitive-behavioral therapy has been tested in numerous controlled studies and has been found to be effective for the treatment of bulimia nervosa and binge-eating disorder. In more than 30 controlled studies of bulimia nervosa, cognitive-behavioral therapy was found more effective than no therapy, non-directive psychotherapy, pill placebo, psychodynamic therapy (supportive-expressive therapy), stress management, and antidepressant medication. Although less is known about the effectiveness of cognitive-behavioral therapy in binge-eating disorder, controlled studies suggest that it is as effective, if not more effective, in the treatment of bulimia nervosa. About half the individuals with bulimia nervosa who complete treatment recover with cognitive-behavioral therapy, and another quarter are much improved. The figures for binge-eating disorder are higher, with 60–70% of those who complete therapy recovering. In the longest follow-up study, Christopher Fairburn and his colleagues at Oxford University followed bulimic patients treated with cognitive-behavioral therapy for 5 years after treatment. Nearly 60% had no eating disorder, and a further 20% now had a sub-clinical disorder with infrequent binge eating and purging at the end of the study period. The remainder had not recovered, with a small percentage diagnosed with anorexia nervosa. Hence, relapse rates for the successfully treated patient are low, although there may be occasional setbacks, and the benefits seem to be long lasting.

Interpersonal psychotherapy was initially used with depressed patients and was later applied to patients with bulimia nervosa and then to those with binge-eating disorder. This treatment is based on the theory that faulty handling of interpersonal relationships causes an emotional upset, which, combined with chronic dieting, will trigger a binge. The combination of hunger and emotional upset is a commonly reported trigger for binge eating. It is much harder to handle your emotions when you are hungry. Despite the overwhelming evidence that cognitive-behavioral therapy is the most effective treatment for bulimia nervosa, a surprising finding in two studies was that IPT, although much less effective than CBT at the end of treatment, was as effective as CBT 1 year after treatment ended. Because of the slower action of IPT, cognitive-behavioral therapy is regarded as the treatment of choice in bulimia nervosa.

Surprisingly, in binge-eating disorder, IPT has been found to be as effective as CBT at the end of treatment and at follow-up. Moreover, treatment gains were well maintained during follow-up. It appears that, at least for cognitive-behavioral therapy (and probably for interpersonal therapy), patients who stop binge eating lose weight, whereas those who do not stop binge eating gain weight. In the longest follow-up study of weight loss in binge-eating disorder, there was a difference of about 15 lbs between those who did not stop binge eating and those who did. This was partly because those who did not stop binge eating put on weight during the follow-up period.

Other Psychotherapies

Dialectical Behavior Therapy

One promising treatment for eating disorders is known as dialectical behavior therapy (DBT). Originally developed to treat patients with personality disorders, DBT works by helping individuals better recognize, understand, and control their emotions. It may be useful in treating binge eating because most people who binge say that negative and upsetting emotions are the most common trigger for their binges. Also, it seems likely that binge eating is a way to avoid strong negative feelings and the consequences of these feelings. Hence, briefer versions of the original DBT treatment were developed specifically for binge eating. Some studies suggest that DBT may be useful to treat both bulimia nervosa and binge-eating disorder, although it has not been compared with cognitive-behavioral therapy. This treatment focuses first on helping individuals recognize their emotional states and see how those emotions lead to binge eating. Then, various skills are taught to help individuals better handle these emotional states. Some of these skills will be covered in the second half of this book.

Psychotherapy with Medication

If medication and psychotherapy are both effective, does combining them lead to better results than using either treatment alone? Theory would suggest that if the two treatments work in different ways, ultimately in the brain, then they should complement one another, and the combination would be better than either one alone. However, if they work in the same way, then there would be no benefit to adding medication to psychotherapy. Several controlled trials have examined this question. The consensus from these studies is that medication adds significantly to the effects of psychotherapy but not nearly as much as psychotherapy adds to the effects of medication. Moreover, in binge-eating disorder, there is little evidence that medication adds to the effectiveness of psychotherapy in reducing binge eating, although it may help a bit with weight loss. This lack of extra effectiveness may be because more people with binge-eating disorder than with bulimia nervosa improve with psychotherapy, so there is less opportunity for medication to demonstrate improvement. In most of the studies combining antidepressant medication and psychotherapy, depression is lowered more effectively with medication than with psychotherapy.

Using Antidepressants in Treatment

There are probably three ways to use medication for bulimia nervosa or binge-eating disorder. Some individuals might not want to spend the time and effort that is necessary in psychotherapy. For these individuals, medication may be a better first choice. Remember though that medication has side effects and that antidepressant medication is not as effective as CBT. Also, it is not clear how long antidepressant treatment should continue before it can be safely withdrawn without relapse. In some cases, medication seems to lose its effectiveness over time. Another option is to add medication to enhance the effects of cognitive-behavioral therapy. One way to do this would be to add medication if there were insufficient progress in the first few weeks of psychotherapy. If individuals have not reduced their purging by 70% or so by the end of six sessions of treatment, they have less chance of doing well than those who show an adequate improvement. This then may be the point at which to add medication. Finally, because depression makes it more difficult to concentrate on getting better with psychotherapy, it makes sense to reduce the depression with antidepressant therapy before beginning CBT.

We have seen that there is firm evidence that cognitive-behavioral therapy should be regarded as the first-line treatment for bulimia nervosa, with interpersonal psychotherapy and medication as second-line treatments. For binge-eating disorder, it seems that both cognitive-behavioral and interpersonal psychotherapy should be regarded as first-line treatments, followed by antidepressant treatment. More recently, short forms of cognitive-behavioral therapy (like the one presented in this workbook) have been developed and have been tested against full CBT. The results of these studies are discussed in the next chapter.

Chapter 5

Evidence for the Effectiveness of Guided Self-Help

Self-help manuals, usually with aid from a qualified mental health professional, have recently become more popular for treating a number of psychological disorders, including eating disorders. The book *Overcoming Binge Eating* by Christopher Fairburn (1995) was the first such manual based on CBT, the most effective treatment for bulimia nervosa and binge-eating disorder. The best way to use a self-help manual is to read the book on your own and attend a few brief sessions with a therapist or clinician trained in CBT. During these sessions, he or she will evaluate your progress, answer any questions, and help you address any stumbling blocks. This method is called guided self-help (GSH).

Studies completed to date suggest that GSH is as effective as full CBT for patients with bulimia nervosa and binge-eating disorder. One of the earliest studies came from London; in it, cognitive-behavioral treatment was compared to guided self-help for patients with bulimia nervosa. In this trial, the treatments were equally effective. In a more recent, larger study, self-help was again tested against cognitive-behavioral therapy and again proved as effective as cognitive-behavioral therapy both at the end of treatment and one year later.

In the largest study to date, involving nearly 300 bulimic patients treated at four different centers across the United States, there was no difference between guided self-help and full-scale cognitive-behavioral therapy. However, there was an indication that some people did better with self-help and some with cognitive-behavioral therapy. Those with more depression and more life problems did better with self-help, whereas those with less depression and fewer life problems did better with cognitive-behavioral therapy. It's a bit puzzling as to why those with more problems did better with briefer treatment. One possibility is that the treatment interfered less with these individuals' lives because there were fewer and shorter treatment sessions in the guided self-help treatment. Being able to do much of the treatment on their own by reading the self-help book may have been more convenient for those with life problems that leave them less time to devote to therapy sessions. In any event, these findings may allow therapists to determine whether self-help or full cognitive-behavioral therapy is best for a particular individual. Alternatively, some therapists might suggest that self-help be used first; if more treatment is needed, the therapist can switch to full cognitive-behavioral therapy.

There have been fewer studies of self-help for binge-eating disorder than for bulimia nervosa, but all of them suggest that self-help is effective in the treatment of binge-eating disorder. A recent study of more than 200 men and women with binge-eating disorder showed that guided self-help was just as effective as full-scale interpersonal psychotherapy at the end of treatment and at 6 months follow-up. (Remember that interpersonal psychotherapy is as effective as CBT in the treatment of binge-eating disorder.) Both therapies achieved about a 60% recovery rate.

There is every reason to believe that GSH is an effective therapy for both bulimia nervosa and binge-eating disorder. It is for this reason that we detail a self-help program in the second half of this workbook.

A Step-by-Step Approach to Treatment

Chapter 6

An Assessment of Your Eating Problems: Is It Time to Begin Treatment?

Goals

- To read and review the entire chapter and discuss with your therapist any questions you might have

- To assess your readiness for treatment by completing and reviewing the Costs and Benefits Analysis exercise

- To make a decision about proceeding or not proceeding with treatment

Before you begin this program, you need to take a long, hard look at yourself and your life circumstances to determine if this is really a good time—the best time—for you to pursue the treatment and resolution of your eating disorder. Typically, the best time to begin a treatment program of this nature is when you can guarantee that it will be your highest priority and that your life will be stable enough to sustain your efforts at treatment. You need to be convinced that the benefits of getting better exceed the costs of staying stuck in your disorder. When you can envision the various ways your life will change if you successfully respond to this program (and the likelihood that things won't change if you don't even try), then it is time to start. You will most likely be motivated to do the hard work required for change when your life circumstances seem stable. On the other hand, if you are starting a new job, moving, getting married, going through a breakup, or beginning some type of educational program, whether high school, college, or postgraduate work, this is unlikely to be the best time for you to start treatment. In any case, to determine that you are ready to begin this program, you need to thoroughly assess yourself and your life circumstances.

Use the form provided to assess your readiness for treatment.

Costs and Benefits Analysis

	Costs	Benefits
Costs and Benefits of Beginning Treatment		
Costs and Benefits of Not Beginning Treatment		

The Initial Evaluation

Use of this guided self-help workbook requires the assistance of a supportive and experienced mental health professional (e.g., a trained counselor, social worker, psychotherapist, psychologist, or psychiatrist). He or she will conduct an initial evaluation of your disorder and help you decide if this is the right treatment for you. If it is, he or she will support you as you use the workbook before, after, in between, and during a series of approximately 8 to 12 sessions of 20 to 25 minutes each. The first four sessions are held once a week for the first 4 weeks of treatment. The remaining sessions can occur every 2 weeks, or even monthly, depending on your needs. Guided self-help sessions like these allow you to use the book as the primary source of information and guidance on the issues and challenges of your eating disorder, while having the supportive presence and gentle prodding of your therapist when you get stuck or have questions. In guided self-help, the goals of overcoming your eating disorder are clear and specific, and each session is used to address an issue related to these goals. This focused drive to overcome your eating problems without the distraction of other concerns—although it may seem quite different from your notions about therapy—is the hallmark of guided self-help.

This workbook was developed based on the findings of the clinical research studies reviewed in Chapter 4 as an alternative to full-scale CBT for patients experiencing the symptoms of either bulimia nervosa or binge-eating disorder. It was conceptualized as a tool for patients to use in a stepwise fashion, mostly as a guidebook to help them learn about their eating-disorder issues and experiment with tools that can help them change. The sessions were viewed as opportunities to check in with a therapist who could expand upon the information in the workbook if necessary and provide additional support and motivation. In guided self-help, the workbook is the primary therapeutic tool. Sessions with a therapist are reinforcements. The content areas are arranged as "steps" that each patient can read and review and then refer back to, as they apply.

The program is cumulative in nature, so each accomplishment is carried forward through all the subsequent work. The first few steps, which are deemed most central or necessary to accomplishing the goals of CBT, include keeping Daily Food Records, regularizing eating, eliminating purging, and weighing oneself weekly. We encourage you to read and review the material in this workbook and to attempt to make and sustain the changes suggested in each step before going on to the next. Mastering any given step could take up to a few weeks, depending on the individual. On the other hand, as improvement and recovery happen, it might become apparent that some of the steps aren't necessary (or that the length or number of sessions can be shortened).

After completing the initial evaluation and introducing the CBT model, your therapist will discuss the various steps of the program as they are presented in this workbook. Whether you suffer from bulimia or binge-eating disorder, your therapist will link these steps to your personalized CBT model, which provides a rationale for the types of behavior changes each step suggests. The two essential tasks of recording your daily intake of food using Daily Food Records and working toward a regularized eating pattern of three meals and two snacks a day are emphasized first. Normalizing your eating is something you will do gradually. Logically, the easiest changes to make (e.g., continuing to eat the solid foods and snacks that you already eat, or adding in those that seem the most doable) should be made first. As the number of regular meals and snacks (approaching three meals and two snacks per day) increases and is maintained, binge eating and compulsive overeating will decrease, as will all types of purging, including vomiting and laxative abuse. Over-exercising may need to be addressed as a separate challenge.

When you are somewhat settled into a more normalized pattern of eating, you will notice that the triggers for your binges are not necessarily based on hunger or cravings but on thoughts, feelings, conflicts, and situations that are less obviously linked to your eating problem. Once your eating patterns are normalized, you will begin to use the tools in this workbook to help you address these triggers. You will use your Daily Food Records (particularly the comments column) to evaluate your binge episodes and what triggered them. It is important to review all the information included on the food record (e.g., the place, time, circumstances, people, and particular food(s) involved, in addition to the thoughts and feelings you experienced before, during, and after the episode) in order to learn from your eating mistakes.

Homework

- ✎ Complete the Costs and Benefits Analysis and examine your readiness for treatment.
- ✎ Talk with your therapist about the advisability of beginning treatment at this time.

Chapter 7   *Understanding and Applying the CBT Model*

Goals

- To read and review the entire chapter and discuss with your therapist any questions you might have

- To review the model for understanding bulimia nervosa and binge-eating disorder

- To work with your therapist to apply the model to your own eating disorder

To help you fully understand all the factors that contribute to maintaining your eating disorder, it is essential that you read and review the information about the CBT model and discuss with your therapist any questions you might have about how it applies specifically to you. By doing this, you will begin to understand in more detail the areas that contribute the most to maintaining your eating disorder.

Understanding the way in which the model works for you will set the stage for carrying out a CBT-based treatment that is not only empirically and theoretically supported and structured but also individualized and tailored to your specific needs. This means that you will have to work hard, by reading and thinking and using your food records to understand the problem areas that contribute the most to your eating disorder. That way, your time in treatment can best be spent addressing those areas rather than focusing on nonessential topics included in the book.

For example, you might be someone who always binges when you have the thought "I feel fat" but never in response to a conflict with a friend, whereas someone else may not binge in response to self-deprecating thoughts but in response to a fight or disagreement with someone close to them. As noted in Chapter 2, the CBT model for eating disorders links low self-esteem, problem moods and emotions, interpersonal conflicts, an overemphasis on maintaining an "ideal" body weight and shape, extreme weight and shape concerns, negative body image, and actual or intended restrictive eating or dieting with out-of-control binge eating and purging (in the case of bulimia). As emphasized earlier, the influences of each of these factors vary according to the individual situation. However, what is most important to remember is that the nuts and bolts of the CBT model *do* apply to everyone with an eating disorder. What this means for those with bulimia is that dieting, restrictive eating, purging, and over-exercising, all of which deplete the body and its fuel stores, eventually contribute to urges to overeat or binge. If you think about it, this is just common sense. If you skip a few meals, starve yourself, and "use up" or "empty" the fuel (food) you have taken in to meet your energy needs and nutritional requirements, your body will simply send you a signal to eat more, to make up the difference. For those with binge-eating disorder, even the *intention* to restrict food intake—and all the *mental* energy that goes into thinking about food and eating and weight and shape—sets the stage for further overeating, often as an attempt to get rid of the bad feelings and moods that result from these negative food- and body-related pressures.

Case Examples

In one instance, a woman in her early 20s moved to the United States, felt "out of it" socially and academically as a result of not knowing the language at first, developed some negative feelings about herself (low self-esteem) as a result, and for that reason became preoccupied with her appearance (she wore glasses and had braces) and her weight. Her weight was on the high end of the normal range and did not reflect the "thin body ideal" of U.S. culture. Her shape, while fit and toned, was not the feminine look she thought men her age were looking for. She focused more and more on her body until she became locked in a cycle of dieting, becoming overly hungry, losing control, and overeating or bingeing, and then purging to rid her body of the excess food and calories, leading to feelings of shame and guilt. Over time, she became entrenched in this bulimic pattern and only some years later came in seeking treatment for it.

Another example is that of a middle-aged, married mother of two who had always carried a bit of extra weight. Although being overweight never bothered her much, she finally sought treatment when her children left for school. During the long hours at home alone, she became aware that her eating and dieting patterns, particularly overeating by grazing throughout the day then making brief and half-hearted attempts to restrict her intake and start a diet, were causing her more distress than her weight was. These behaviors, in addition to contributing to weight gain and potentially having a negative effect on her teenage daughter, were also causing her a great deal of distress and shame. She would make decisions to avoid social gatherings after she overate or at times when she "felt fat," and would continually demean herself when she observed her loss of control over food. She finally sought treatment when she realized she didn't want to live this way anymore. She wanted to be more available to her husband and her children and in all respects to begin to enjoy her life.

Your Eating Disorder

No matter what your reasons for seeking treatment, it is essential that you use this workbook and your therapist's help to identify and understand what specifically contributes to your disordered eating behaviors and associated issues. After you discuss with your therapist the CBT model as it applies to your situation, you will understand even more about the issues presently maintaining your eating disorder. Even more important, you will now be in a position to start using Daily Food Records to understand more about the factors that are maintaining your eating disorder. You must first accept the fact that your pattern of actual or intended restriction, such as skipping meals, eliminating certain foods from your diet, eating only very small meals and snacks, and so on, has maintained your eating disorder by leading to out-of-control eating and purging (in some cases). Only then will you also understand why it is so important to commit to working toward a pattern of regular meals and snacks. According to this theory, disrupting your pattern of under-eating is the key to overcoming your eating disorder. Once you accept the CBT model, the next step involves making a commitment to complete your Daily Food Records to obtain as much information as you can about the specifics of your eating patterns. Don't worry; your therapist will review your first set of records with you in your session to make sure you are completing them correctly and interpreting the information in the most productive way. Over time, if you accept the model, you will continue to work toward a regular pattern of eating to get rid of the primary contributor to your eating problems: namely, hunger and deprivation. Daily Food Records are the first step in this treatment and are described in more detail in the following chapter.

Homework

✎ Work with your therapist to personalize the CBT model of binge eating as it applies to you.

Chapter 8   *Using Daily Food Records to Monitor Eating*

Goals

- To read and review the entire chapter and discuss with your therapist any questions you might have
- To begin using Daily Food Records to monitor your eating patterns

Importance of Food Records

If you are struggling with either bulimia nervosa or binge-eating disorder, it may be that you lack the tool of "self-observation," or awareness. What this means is that you probably don't remember, acknowledge, or understand many of the details of or reasons behind specific instances of problem eating. You probably also overlook the factors associated with experiences of "good eating" so that you also don't really know what works to keep you on track. We recommend keeping very detailed food records so that you stay aware of the many factors associated with your eating patterns. Through the process of maintaining these food records, you will be able to distance yourself from your behavior and gain perspective while also learning about the specific factors that make your eating problems better or worse.

Although you may have used food records in some capacity before starting this treatment and found that they did not work for you, we want to emphasize that in *this* program your food records will be used in an altogether different manner. The emphasis will not be on calorie counting or "dieting" but rather on eliminating dieting and normalizing your eating so that your daily eating routine begins to resemble a more regular pattern of three meals and two snacks per day.

What Is a Daily Food Record?

The Daily Food Record provides space to write about your various eating experiences, whether these are episodes of healthy eating or instances of bingeing, purging, dieting, and so on.

Daily Food Record Instructions

At first, writing down everything you eat may well be irritating and inconvenient, but soon it will become second nature and obviously valuable. We have yet to encounter anyone whose lifestyle makes monitoring truly impossible. You may photocopy the relevant Daily Food Record from the workbook or download multiple copies from the Treatments *That Work*™ Web site at www.oup.com/us/ttw. We have provided two blank copies, one for use by those with bulimia and one for use by those with binge-eating disorder. Please use the one that applies to you.

Use a new record (or records) each day, noting the date and day of the week in the space provided. Make entries as soon as possible after eating. It is not helpful to try to remember later what you ate or drank hours before.

Column 1 of the Daily Food Record is for noting the time when you eat or drink anything during the day. Column 2 is for recording the type and amount of the food and liquid consumed. Do not record calories. Instead, provide a simple description of what you ate or drank. Remember that one of the two purposes of monitoring is to help you change. Obviously, if you are to record your food intake in this way, you will have to carry your monitoring sheets with you. Meals should be identified with parentheses. A meal may be defined as "a discrete episode of eating that was controlled, organized, and eaten in a 'normal' fashion." List, but don't use parentheses for snacks and other eating episodes.

Column 3 is for recording where you were when you consumed the food or liquid. If you were at home, write down which room you were in. If you were at work, describe your exact location (e.g., sit-

Daily Food Record for Bulimic Patients

Time	Food and Liquid Consumed	Location	Binge?	Purge?	Comments

Daily Food Record for Binge-Eating Patients

Time	Food and Liquid Consumed	Location	Binge?	Exercise	Comments

ting at your desk, in the cafeteria, etc.). Column 4 is for indicating whether or not you felt the eating episode was excessive and constituted a binge. Put a checkmark in the column if you considered it a binge. It is essential to record all the food you eat during any overeating episodes or binges. Column 5 is for recording when you vomit or take laxatives or water pills. If you have binge-eating disorder, you will use Column 5 to record your exercise.

Use Column 6 as a diary to record events or situations that influenced your eating. For example, if it seemed that an argument might have precipitated a binge, you should make note of it in that column. You may wish to record other important events as well, even if they had no effect on your eating. It is also a good idea to write down any strong feelings such as depression, anxiety, boredom, or loneliness, or feelings of "fatness" that you think might have contributed to your eating behavior. In addition, use Column 6 to record your weight each time you weigh yourself.

Each one of your sessions will include a review of your latest food records. It is very important that you remember to bring them with you.

We have provided two sample completed Daily Food Records (Figures 8.1 and 8.2) to illustrate the types of eating problems typical of a person with bulimia and a person with binge-eating disorder.

How to Read Your Food Record for Maximum Learning

To get the most benefit from your food records, it is important that you review and evaluate your completed records correctly. The first step for now is to review your overall eating pattern. It is helpful to review your records daily to determine whether a particular day was a good or not-so-good day and why or why not. It is helpful to rate each day as "good" or "needing improvement" and to note this at the top of that day's record. A good day may be one where you noticed an improvement in the way you feel or in any of your problem eating behaviors, such as a decrease in purging episodes. A bad day may be one where you felt out of control and engaged in large or multiple binges.

Time	Food and Liquid Consumed*	Location	Binge?	Purge?	Comments
8:00 am	1 cup Coffee, half a banana	Kitchen			I was rushed
11:15 am	Nestle chocolate bar	Desk			Bought it a few days ago and left in my desk, bad but easy.
2:15 pm	Kraft Mac and Cheese, Diet Coke-half a can	Desk			Couldn't get out for lunch, not excessive eating but not good for me either
6:00 pm	2 wafer cookies with chocolate filling	Desk			
7:30 pm	4 KFC spicy breaded chicken strips, 1/4 cup of BBQ beans, 2 cups of corn with butter, 2 biscuits, ranch dressing, 1 pint of ice cream	In front of TV	Binge	Vomited	Had a quarrel with my boyfriend on the phone before this. Felt angry and resentful.

Figure 8.1 Example of Completed Daily Food Record for Bulimic Patient

Next, to examine the details of your eating, you might note how many regular meals (out of the recommended three) and how many snacks (up to three) you consumed. After determining both, note the time sequencing. Did you eat your meals and snacks at regular intervals? For each instance of undesirable eating (e.g., skipping meals and/or snacks, or purging), note the associated factors by looking at what you've recorded in the comments column of your record.

Resistance to Record Keeping

Usually, when individuals exhibit some form of resistance to the idea of using food records (other than having tried them unsuccessfully before), it is related to fears of losing control over their eating and thereby gaining weight. Many individuals unnecessarily fear that weight gain is a natural consequence of adopting the regular pattern

Time	Food and Liquid Consumed*	Location	Binge?	Exercise	Comments
7:45 am	2 slices of bread with jam	kitchen		10 minute walk	A little hungry, just wanted to eat enough to last to lunch time
10:30 am	1 can Diet Pepsi				
11:30 am	8 thin mints, 2 cups of cheese nips, 3 pieces of pizza, 2 glasses of water	office	Binge		Started with the cookies, it's hopeless! I really don't like working here. I am out of control. I'll never lose weight
1:30 pm	15 Hershey's Kisses	office	Binge		Falling asleep, need sugar or something, don't want this, I'm not hungry
6:30 pm	2 thick peanut butter sandwiches, 2 glasses of milk				I want to stuff myself, out of control. I'm getting tired of this. I am alone.

Figure 8.2 Example of Completed Daily Food Record for Binge-Eating Patient

of eating advocated by the model (and those who do use records correctly are more likely to adopt this recommended pattern). If you struggle with bulimia, you may not believe it is possible to establish and sustain a regular eating pattern while also maintaining your weight in a comfortable range. On the other hand, if you have binge-eating disorder, you might not believe that it is possible to manage your emotions without overeating, especially if bingeing has been one of your primary strategies for self-soothing and comforting.

A regular pattern of eating for a binge eater may feel like, and represent, a *reduction* in food intake. Alternatively, normalized eating in bulimics will likely represent an *increase* in food intake. If you are a binge eater, you may fear that not having free access to food will result in feelings of hunger, deprivation, and anxiety. You might even recognize that in the past you have resisted treatment by superficially complying with the recommendation to structure your eating patterns while in actuality simply eating abnormally large quantities of food at these set meals or snacks. If you have binge-eating disorder, you and your therapist need to explore any feelings of deprivation that surface as you attempt to control your food intake. These feelings might be difficult to discern, but your feeling a certain level of inexplicable emotional distress as you work on your food issues in the sessions with your therapist might be one clue.

On the other hand, if you have a problem with bulimia, you are more likely to subtly resist the treatment recommendations by eating much less than you should at scheduled meals and snacks because you fear weight gain. Resistance might also take the form of continuing to purge, using subtle and easily disguised tactics such as excessive exercise.

Homework

- Begin to regularize your eating by consuming three meals and two snacks per day.
- Complete Daily Food Records for the remainder of today and every day until your next therapy session.

Chapter 9

Establishing a Regular Pattern of Eating Plus Weekly Weighing

Goals

- To read and review the entire chapter and discuss with your therapist any questions you might have

- To work toward establishing a regular pattern of eating

- To begin weighing yourself weekly

Establishing a regular pattern of eating is the most powerful step you can take toward overcoming your eating disorder. For those with long-standing eating disorders, establishing a regular pattern of three meals and two snacks per day, eaten at regular intervals, can be one of the most immediate and gratifying symptom-reducing strategies. At the very same time, however, this crucial behavior change is much more difficult to accomplish than you or those around you may think. In addition to being afraid of losing control over your food intake and then gaining weight, you may encounter many other obstacles as you take small steps toward establishing a regular eating pattern. These barriers might include the presence of rigid and ingrained eating habits and patterns, some of which might inappropriately appear to promise "safety" or have nearly "magical" qualities in terms of keeping your eating on track and your weight in a manageable range. Although these behaviors and attitudes will vary from person to person, some examples include skipping breakfast or consuming only diet sodas, water, and black coffee in the morning and/or delaying eating until as late in the day as possible (which is highly likely to lead to bingeing). Or you might be hypersensitive to certain bodily sensations associated with normal eating and normal feelings of fullness. For example, if you have bulimia, you might experience any form of stomach fullness as excessive "bloating" and therefore interpret it to mean automatic weight gain rather than viewing it as a natural and necessary consequence of eating regular meals and snacks. Some of you might cite "circumstances" (such as time constraints) to explain why you don't want to, or can't, eat regularly. Or you might attribute your avoidance of regular eating, particularly in public, to feelings of shame and embarrassment about others' seeing you eat.

If you are suffering from binge eating of any type—with or without purging—you should expect that regularizing your meal pattern will present a challenge and may take some time to achieve. Of course, the level of difficulty will depend on the specifics of your eating. Completing the cost–benefit analysis at the beginning of this workbook clearly showed you that you chose this active treatment and saw it as appropriate. Therefore, it is likely you selected this treatment for all the right reasons, including your willingness to stay motivated, committed, and ready and available for this guided self-help program. With that in mind, you should rarely if ever experience huge lapses in motivation or an unwillingness to at least try to change.

The method for working toward normalizing your eating patterns involves a "small steps" approach. It is probably better to focus first on meals instead of snacks because the former provide the anchors to your overall eating plan. Committing first to eating three meals a day helps you avoid falling into a grazing pattern (excessive snacking) over a period of hours or days.

When you first start making changes and improvements in your eating pattern, minding the content and the quantity of the meal or snack you're adding in is much less important than normalizing the pattern so that the time between eating episodes is no longer than 4 hours and no shorter than 2. In terms of content, you need to pay careful attention to those foods that have previously triggered overeating, bingeing, or purging. Also, you must commit to eating somewhat more than "starvation portions" but not overdoing it. In a later step, you will work on your relationship with the foods you fear and avoid, which may be those that end up triggering cravings or binges. An example of an early therapy goal for a bulimic who might be skipping breakfast and/or lunch is to eat *something* during at least one of those important meal times and to slowly work toward consuming normal-sized meals.

Most likely, you will quickly begin to feel comfortable completing and reviewing your food records daily, and you will find these records are essential because they provide you with all the important information about your eating patterns, help you stay motivated and on track, and can serve as a source of "intervention" to steer you toward healthy choices when you are tempted to revert to a problem behavior.

Beginning a Healthy Weighing Routine

Additionally, you will be asked to weigh yourself once a week. Eating-disordered individuals tend to adopt one of two patterns of weighing, best characterized as compulsive or avoidant. The compulsive types weigh themselves excessively and may step on the scale up to several times per day, often after meals and again after using the bathroom, setting themselves up to feel demoralized in response to normal and insignificant changes in weight. Avoidant types tend to shun the scale but seem to have some sense of their weight range and typically exaggerate changes in their weight following bouts of overeating or dieting. In both cases, there is a heightened sensitivity to the importance and meaning of the numbers on the scale.

It will be helpful to keep track of your weight as you make changes in your eating behaviors (including cutting down on binge eating and purging, if you are bulimic). Tracking your weight enables you to better understand the *real* relationship between your intake, your activity patterns, and your weight, correcting your belief in more arbitrary relationships (e.g., that purging, sweating a lot, or maintaining a flat stomach affects weight over the long term). You can record your weight in the comments column of your Daily Food Record and/or use the weight graph on page 57. You should speak with your therapist about any difficulties you have establishing a weekly weighing pattern, and he or she will assist you in applying all the tools you need to accomplish this important goal.

Corrective Strategies: Weekly Weighing and Other Measurements

A helpful strategy to address problem patterns of weighing is to plan to weigh yourself regularly, such as once a week on a specific day, at a specific time. Weighing regularly is the way to get accurate data to compare week to week. If you have been weighing yourself compulsively, establishing a regular pattern of weighing is the best strategy for helping you stop. For example, once you select a day and a time for weighing, you can make the scale "off-limits," either by putting it in a closet or a hard-to-reach place, or by limiting access to it by taking out the batteries or hanging a sign as a reminder to stay away from it. If you weigh yourself excessively outside your home, you may need to use problem-solving methods and motivational exercises (e.g., completing a cost–benefit analysis) to help you limit visits to the weighing location to your once-weekly weigh-in day. In addition, relaxation, distraction, and cognitive-restructuring methods might help you address any anxiety or other problem moods on the days when weighing is not an option.

The strategy of committing to a specific day and time also applies to those who avoid the scale entirely. If you fall into this category, you may need to either purchase an appropriate scale for your home or identify a location where you can easily access a scale once a week on a specific day at a specific time. You may also need to supplement weekly weighing with problem-solving strategies, relaxation exercises (to combat anxiety that might occur before, during, and/or after you weigh yourself), and cognitive-restructuring exercises to challenge any negative thoughts you may have when you see the numbers on the scale.

Later chapters in this workbook discuss problem-solving techniques, cognitive-restructuring strategies, and relaxation exercises.

A weekly weight chart can help you maintain a visual image of your progress toward weight loss. In your session with your therapist, you can set up your weight graph in a form that will be most helpful to you.

As you become more skilled in maintaining a regular pattern of eating three meals and two snacks a day, your eating behavior patterns will improve. For bulimic patients, there will be a noticeable decrease

My Weight Graph

Note: You can either use this graph to track your weight over a 30-day period (e.g., a month), or you can otherwise assign meaningful numbers to the cells (e.g., each cell representing 1 week or 5 pounds) to keep track of your weight.

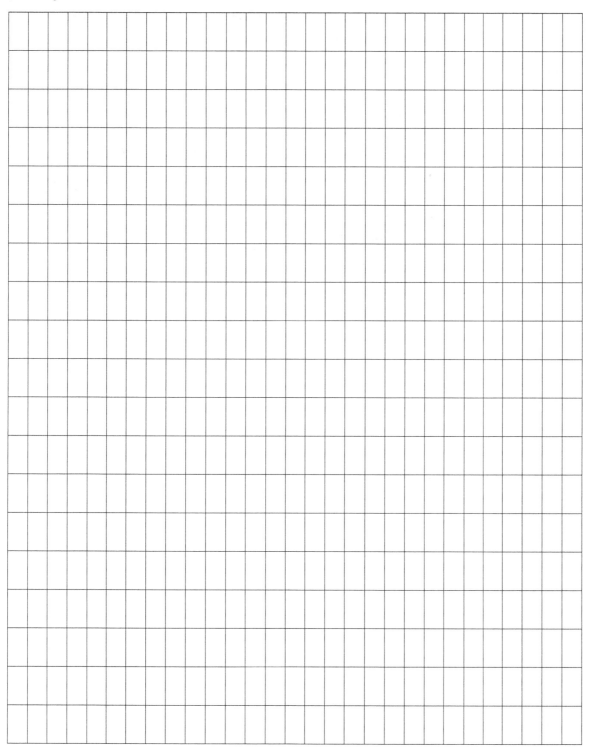

in the frequency of both binge and purge episodes. For binge-eating patients, the frequency of grazing, bingeing, or otherwise grossly overeating will also decrease. For both groups, by design, a regular eating pattern will disrupt long periods of going without food, which is a form of restricting that can trigger a binge.

Homework

- Continue working toward a regular pattern of eating.
- Continue self-monitoring by keeping Daily Food Records.
- Establish a regular weighing regimen. Decide on a given time and place, and plan activities for afterward.
- Record your weight for the week and any associated thoughts or feelings in the comments column of your Daily Food Record and/or on the weight graph.

Chapter 10   *Feared and Problem Foods*

Goals

- To read and review the entire chapter and discuss with your therapist any questions you might have

- To visit a grocery store and create a list of foods you fear and/or avoid

- To begin incorporating your least feared foods into your daily eating routine

    It is quite likely that you have developed a complicated relationship with at least some foods that you currently or formerly liked, or even craved. It might be that you have made efforts to limit your intake of certain foods, to avoid temptation or losing control if you eat just a little. You might have made some erroneous assumptions about given foods (or food groups). For example, you might assume that these foods automatically lead to weight gain or other undesirable outcomes for your body, appearance, or health. Common feared foods for many bulimics, and in some cases binge eaters, include cookies, chocolate, baked goods or sweets, chips, cheese, and pizza, among others. You might follow vegetarian or vegan philosophies and practices for philosophical, political, or religious reasons. Although this treatment approach does not set out to challenge your belief system about eating, it will require that you stay open to questioning some of your assumptions about certain foods that you have been avoiding in order to definitively rule out (or acknowledge) the influence of your eating disorder on your choices.

    The intervention outlined in this chapter involves helping you actively attempt to modify your relationship to your trigger foods. Though it may seem counterintuitive, the strategy for accomplishing this involves your eventually learning to incorporate some of your feared foods into your diet.

Identifying Feared Foods

Ideally, you should complete this exercise at a grocery store, where you can easily be reminded of the many types of foods you automatically label as bad or off-limits. The initial objective is to heighten your awareness of the extent to which you avoid particular foods. First, take a notebook and pen to the store and note all the feared or off-limits foods you notice. Make sure you go to the store to do this when you are not at great risk for binge eating or purging, so that the act of surrounding yourself with feared foods and thinking about them in depth does not in and of itself trigger a binge.

In addition to visiting the grocery store, you should also take an inventory of the fast-food establishments and other restaurants that you have frequented (possibly with trepidation), whether before developing your eating disorder, during a binge, or during occasional attempts to "eat normally." This step will help you include the foods you encounter in those settings so that you will not omit any problem items from your list.

In completing this task, it is important that you really think through all the foods and not brush off or dismiss as unimportant any food items. For example, a thought such as "That's not something that I even like at all or would ever eat; it's not healthy" might incline you to leave that item off your list. Instead, it is better if you really challenge yourself to look at the possibility that there *might* be a connection between your disinterest in or dismissal of this particular food and your eating disorder, even if you have not eaten the food in question in a very long time. For example, some individuals with eating disorders might have sworn off burgers and fries long ago but still crave them on occasion or even purchase them as binge foods when at a restaurant or in the frozen or prepared-foods section of the grocery store.

Organizing Your List

The next part of this exercise involves taking the list of foods and categorizing them according to the degree of anxiety or trepidation you experience when you think about having some as part of a regu-

Feared and Problem Foods List

Category 1 (least feared)	Category 2	Category 3	Category 4 (most feared)

lar meal or snack (not a binge). Use the Feared and Problem Foods List provided to group the foods into four categories. Category 1 represents foods you fear the least, and Category 4 represents foods you fear the most. A Category 1 food is a food you've tried to limit but not avoid altogether. A Category 4 food is a food that, when you think about adding it to your diet, causes you great anxiety because you feel you can't eat it without going overboard. Categories 2 and 3 represent foods that you find somewhat difficult to add to your diet; they fall somewhere in the middle range in terms of the amount of anxiety they create for you.

Introducing Feared Foods into Your Diet

Once you have organized your list of feared foods according to the relative anxiety you feel when you think about eating them, your next task is to begin to slowly add small portions of these foods to meals or snacks. The goal of this exercise is not to pressure you or force you to eat any of these foods on a daily, weekly, or even twice-monthly basis. Rather, the point is to help you develop a flexible and masterful relationship to these foods so that if you are presented with any of them in a given situation, you can consume a small portion comfortably without anxiety and without losing control. In addition, this exercise should help you neutralize these foods so that they don't further contribute to feelings of deprivation or cravings, which are the kinds of feelings that might have caused you to binge on them in the past.

Generally, it is best if you start with the least feared foods on your list (Category 1) before moving on to those that are more challenging. On the other hand, you may find that simply starting to play around with the idea that you can confront your feared foods and begin to eat them again motivates you to take some of these on spontaneously in a variety of unexpected settings and situations. Whether you have a feared-foods exercise planned or are spontaneously confronted with a challenging food opportunity, it is essential that you determine that you are in the *right frame of mind* and in the *right type of situation* to succeed with your eating goal.

You need to pay careful attention to your feelings and thoughts in deciding whether or not it is safe to proceed. If you feel you are at risk for problem eating in *any way* for *any reason* (e.g., you are upset or in a bad mood, you recently had a fight with someone close to you, the amount of the feared food that you are faced with is very large), you need to postpone the exercise and do your food exposure at another time. For example, if you wanted to experiment with having one or two medium-sized cookies in the controlled environment of a work meeting, but earlier that day, while in a bad mood and feeling fat, you were confronted with a freshly baked batch of cookies at the store, it would be best to postpone the cookie experiment. In other words, to safely experiment with any of your feared foods, you need to be feeling calm and not distressed by anything, including concerns about your body, recent conflicts with other people, large amounts of available food, or a sense that you will inevitably binge. It is helpful to imagine treating the feared food as a delicacy, while in the presence of a respected guest, a supportive friend, or a loved one. Picture yourself with that special person, eating a reasonable amount of the food in a safe, relaxed, and comfortable situation, perhaps sharing a piece of decadent cake at a restaurant where you've gone together for dessert. This image is a much more calming and hopeful than contemplating "going it alone" in a situation in which you might be overwhelmed.

It is also important to attend to "stimulus control" when you are modifying your eating to overcome an eating disorder. In addition to the feared foods that you have struggled to avoid or eat in moderation, you may be aware of certain eating *situations* that are more likely to result in problematic eating episodes. Managing your eating patterns involves identifying and then eliminating eating that occurs in situations or locations that should not naturally include food. For example, you shouldn't eat in your car, at your desk, or while working at your computer, reading in bed, or taking a bath. Each time you eat in one of these places or situations that is inherently inappropriate for eating, you strengthen an association between that situation or place and the act of eating. Eventually, you may want food whenever you find yourself in similar situations or places, even though you aren't necessarily hungry.

Places of Eating Inventory

	Yes	No

Home
    In front of TV (couch or other seating) _____ _____

    Bedroom (bed or other) _____ _____

    Bathtub (or bathroom) _____ _____

    Garage _____ _____

    Home office (at desk or other seating) _____ _____

    Car _____ _____

    _____ _____ _____

    _____ _____ _____

    _____ _____ _____

At Work or at School
    Eating or snacking at your desk _____ _____

    Grabbing food at someone else's desk _____ _____

    Snacking between classes _____ _____

    _____ _____ _____

    _____ _____ _____

    _____ _____ _____

Other
    While working in the garden _____ _____

    While walking the dog _____ _____

    While waiting in any line _____ _____

    _____ _____ _____

    _____ _____ _____

    _____ _____ _____

Use the Places of Eating Inventory provided to evaluate the extent of your eating in non-eating situations or places. Check the appropriate column for each location or situation listed. Next, set goals that involve limiting your eating to traditional settings, like the kitchen or dining-room table or the breakfast bar. Also, always try to sit down and eat in a relaxed fashion (rather than eating while standing, or "on the go"). Since it takes 20 minutes for fullness to register in your brain and stomach, it is always best to take your time while eating; this can stave off the possibility of your eating more than you actually need.

When you begin experimenting with feared foods and eating only in appropriate settings, write about your experiences in your Daily Food Record. You will obviously want to make special note of the feared food(s) consumed and use the comments column to specifically address the thoughts and feelings you had before, during, and after your "eating experiment." When you weigh yourself, as you have been doing weekly, you will recognize that eating your feared foods in moderation does not automatically lead to continued weight gain. Commonly, those with eating disorders who have become comfortable eating certain of their feared foods report that they begin to experience a feeling of mastery and control. This happens as they realize that they *can* eat some of these desired or craved but avoided foods in moderate portions without losing control or gaining weight.

Homework

- Continue working toward a regular pattern of eating.
- Continue self-monitoring by keeping Daily Food Records and weighing yourself weekly.
- Create your list of feared foods, grouping the foods into four categories ranging from the least feared to the most feared.
- Include one or two of the least feared foods into your diet this week.

Chapter 11 *Body-Image Concerns*

Goals

- To read and review the entire chapter and discuss with your therapist any questions you might have

- To discuss your concerns about weight and shape and the role they play in your eating disorder

- To learn methods for identifying, monitoring, and reducing the types of body-checking behaviors you perform each day

How do you think and feel about your body? You might be aware that your perception of your body varies somewhat, even over the course of a day. You might start off the day feeling thin and in shape, and then in response to overeating, eating anything at all, seeing numbers on the scale that you think are higher than they should be, or finding that your clothes are tighter, you might begin to feel "fat" or less positive about your body. Negative feelings about your body also might come about in response to other stressors, such as disagreements with people, job frustrations, or daily hassles of one type or another. Alternatively, after a long session at the gym, you might feel differently about your body; you may view yourself as relatively strong, thinner, on the road to fitness, and in control of your food intake and your body.

In any case, it is likely that many experiences in your life have contributed to the way you feel about your body. You will recall reading about this in part in Chapter 2, which discussed the CBT model. You might want to keep all those contributions in mind as you work through this chapter.

Concerns about your body shape usually lead to some form of checking, such as often looking in mirrors, windows, or other reflective surfaces; pinching various areas of your body, such as the upper arms, forearms, or thighs; and trying on various items of clothing to see how they fit. If you are actively and regularly engaging in any of these behaviors, it is quite likely you have never given much thought to how such checking affects your thoughts, feelings, and/or behaviors. Well, now is the time! As you do so, you will probably begin to notice that this type of checking has a negative effect on your state of mind. You will likely notice some negative effects on your self-perceptions, mood, and actions (including decisions you might make to eat to excess, to purge, or to over-exercise).

The place to start when tracking how you evaluate your body is to note exactly what you have been doing to monitor your body in both healthy ways (e.g., weighing yourself once a week and noticing a change in how clothes feel) and negative ways (e.g., excessively measuring certain body parts or weighing yourself too frequently). The best way to do this is to keep a log of the various types of body checking you perform and how many times you perform each behavior. Many people have been quite surprised to realize they are pinching their upper arms or checking some other body part to see "how fat they are" up to 20 times a day. Clearly, their weight or shape could not have changed dramatically, if at all, within one day. Once you collect information about your typical body-checking behaviors, you can begin to explore the thoughts, feelings, and behaviors that are likely to follow from these behaviors.

Record your body-checking data on the form provided as you notice these behaviors over the next couple of weeks or so. Make a tally mark each time you engage in each behavior on each of the 7 days in the upcoming week.

What to Do About Checking

As you observe the thoughts and feelings associated with body checking, you will probably realize that checking is more often associated with negative thoughts and feelings than with anything positive. In other words, checking does not make you feel better about your body. The simplest approach to getting rid of these behaviors is to stop doing them. Some people find it easier to stop all at once; oth-

Body Checking Behaviors

Body Checking Behaviors

1. _____
2. _____
3. _____
4. _____
5. _____
6. _____
7. _____
8. _____

Frequency of Body Checking Behaviors

Behaviors	Mon	Tues	Wed	Thurs	Fri	Sat	Sun
1. _____							
2. _____							
3. _____							
4. _____							
5. _____							
6. _____							

ers prefer to gradually phase out the various behaviors, working to end them one by one over a couple of weeks. If you do it this way, make sure to keep track of each behavior in your log.

Keep in mind, however, that decreasing certain forms of excessive body-checking behavior does not mean stopping healthy strategies for staying in touch with what is happening with your body. For example, weekly weighing sessions and occasionally taking note of how certain items of clothing fit are relatively common, acceptable behaviors. Only rigid and excessive body-checking behaviors pose problems. On the other hand, completely denying any bodily changes can also lead to difficulties.

Homework

- Continue all aspects of the program (keeping Daily Food Records, working toward a regular pattern of eating, and incorporating feared foods into your diet). Continue also to weigh yourself weekly.

- If applicable, begin keeping track of your body-checking behaviors and how frequently you engage in them.

Chapter 12   *Handling Intense Moods and Emotions*

Goals

- To read and review the entire chapter and discuss with your therapist any questions you might have

- To review the role of intense emotions in triggering your problem eating episodes

- To create a list of pleasurable alternative activities incompatible with eating

In addition to hunger, intense mood states may trigger binge eating. The contribution of moods and emotions to problem eating episodes can be particularly strong in individuals who generally have difficulty regulating their emotions. Positive emotions, such as euphoria, enthusiasm, or happiness, and negative emotions, such as anxiety, panic, sadness, loneliness, or emptiness, can lead to episodes of problem eating and/or purging when other tools for problem solving, self-soothing, or coping have not been well developed. Relying on disordered eating to regulate strong emotions can be particularly striking in those who have at any time overused other external forms of mood control. Using alcohol or drugs, being promiscuous, compulsively shopping, or engaging in other self-injurious behaviors, such as cutting or burning, are examples of external forms of mood control. These behaviors often are gratifying in the short term because they can distract a person from the intense emotions they might otherwise feel. The long-term consequences are not ideal and may even be quite negative. Usually, an over-reliance on any of these external solutions simply leads one to rely on them again and again.

The cycle connecting emotional distress and problem eating behavior can take different forms. An individual with an eating disorder might feel compelled to overeat. What this really means is that they are indirectly "choosing" to distract themselves from their intense mood state by engaging in a discrete binge-eating episode, possibly followed by purging (for bulimics). On the other hand, they might engage in an episode of overeating lasting for hours or for an entire day in response to the emotions. Excessive, strenuous exercise might also help control emotions.

Regardless, it is important for you to learn how to analyze situations so that you can trace the intense, triggering mood state back to its origins and in that way work toward a real, permanent solution. Usually, if you trace the chain of events all the way back, you will uncover a place, situation, or series of events (thoughts, feelings, interactions, environments, etc.) that gradually unfolded to upset you. Eventually, you can find ways to interrupt the problem moods and behaviors earlier in the chain. Without becoming aware of these types of links, it will be difficult to modify those circumstances that make you most vulnerable to the emotions that trigger your eating problems. The comments column of the food record provides an ideal opportunity for expanding on and analyzing the connections between your feelings and your eating behaviors. Although the goal is to help you overcome your *problem* eating behaviors, clarifying the relationships between situations, emotions, and eating behaviors can also help you better understand what is going on when you are able to adhere to *healthy* eating patterns.

It is likely that as you analyze your own situation you will recognize at least some links among negative situations, emotions, thoughts, and behavior from the CBT model presented earlier. For example, you find that exposure to a situation that emphasizes our culture's "thin ideal" leads to negative thoughts and feelings about your physical appearance, body weight, or shape that ultimately trigger a binge. On the other hand, you might discover that you begin to struggle with issues of low self-esteem when you've paid too much attention to the media's portrayal of the "ideal body" and that that leads to the problem behaviors. Or, it might be that exposure to others' comments about physical appearance and body shape, arguments with your loved ones, or general interpersonal stressors lead to negative thoughts and emotions, and problem eating behaviors. In any case, the goal of this chapter is to educate you about a variety of emotion-regulation tools that are easy to apply in a variety of situations that might otherwise lead to an intensification of emotion and, eventually, to disordered eating.

Tools for Emotion Regulation and Distress Tolerance

Once you have identified the types of problem emotions associated with your eating-disordered behaviors, you can learn to minimize the "vulnerability" factors that might contribute to your falling into these poor mood states to begin with. Then, as you continue to decrease the effects of these factors on your eating, you will also be able to learn a set of tools and strategies to work through these problem emotions when they do emerge.

Vulnerability factors are easy to explain and understand. Mostly, they have to do with the idea of "being run down"—from fatigue, illness, stress, and poor self-care in any form (eating too little, sleeping too little, drinking too much, working too hard, socializing minimally, getting inadequate physical exercise). Reducing your vulnerability factors means paying attention to, and rectifying, all of the above. Once you minimize the vulnerability factors in your life, you are likely to experience fewer emotional meltdowns of the type that can trigger binge eating. You can easily note the vulnerability factors that you suspect might be responsible for contributing to an episode of disordered eating in the comments column of your Daily Food Record, when you write about the situation in which the poor eating occurred. In the space provided, you can also list the most common vulnerability factors that affect you.

My Most Common Vulnerability Factors:

_____

_____

_____

_____

Once you identify and attempt to eliminate certain of your primary vulnerability factors, the intense, negative emotions you experience will likely decrease in frequency.

Pleasurable Alternative Activities

Effectively managing your risk factors involves refocusing on some alternative, distracting, and pleasurable activity incompatible with binge eating. Even making the effort to engage in an alternative activity tends to push troubling thoughts and feelings into the background, allowing for a fresh and more optimistic perspective. This can be very helpful as you work to overcome the urge to binge. Your challenge then is to create a list of pleasurable and distracting alternative activities that can help keep you from falling victim to some of the emotional influences that make you binge.

Although it may sound simple, creating this list is quite a challenge. Commonly, bulimics report difficulty coming up with activities for this list. They acknowledge having spent an increasing amount of their time over the years involved in eating and related activities and may have a hard time getting in touch with former interests and hobbies. When asked for a list of alternatives, bulimics tend to include aversive activities such as completing household chores like doing laundry or paying bills. Given the types of activities that tend to appear on their lists, it isn't hard to understand why binge eating would appear the more desirable option!

The goal of this exercise is to compile a list of pleasurable alternative activities that can compete with your urge to binge. Physically engaging activities may work best, perhaps because, to the degree that they diffuse tension and stress, they are able to mimic the beneficial effects of binge eating and purging. Other soothing activities may involve an "indulgence," such as taking a hot bubble bath, watching a movie, or getting a massage. Again, the objective in creating this type of list is to distract oneself from the negative thoughts and emotions that might trigger an urge to binge and purge. List your alternative activities in the space provided, keep it handy, and feel free to add to it at any time!

1. _____
2. _____
3. _____
4. _____
5. _____
6. _____
7. _____
8. _____
9. _____
10. _____

Homework

✎ Continue all aspects of the program (keeping Daily Food Records, working toward a regular pattern of eating, and incorporating feared foods into your diet). Continue also to weigh yourself weekly.

✎ Develop a list of pleasurable alternative activities and participate in at least one during the week.

Chapter 13

Working Through Problem Situations and Thoughts

Goals

- To read and review the entire chapter and discuss with your therapist any questions you might have

- To learn effective methods for problem solving and challenging negative thoughts

When faced with a dilemma of any type in which eating or overeating might have emerged as the solution in the past, in addition to using the tools you've learned thus far (e.g., engaging in pleasant alternative activities that are incompatible with eating), you might also consider engaging in formal problem solving. Problem solving is something that many people are able to do naturally and automatically, without giving it much, if any, thought. It might be something you are also able to do quite easily in many, if not most, situations in which you are not stressed or overtaxed in any sense. For example, if you wake up on a given morning and it is cold and rainy, you are probably able to think through your options about what to wear and to easily come up with the solution of wearing warmer clothing and a raincoat and taking an umbrella.

If your problem-solving skills are basically good, then it is probably only in very stressful or complicated situations that you get rattled and for that reason become confused about what you want or how to go about getting what you want. It might be that many of those stressful or confusing situations ultimately involve food in one way or another, either as the only solution or as a delay or a distraction when a solution appears to be too difficult or complicated to implement easily. When eating and food is used in this way, it also serves to regulate your mood, in that it modulates any stress you might feel about the problem you are facing and the challenge of implementing any of the complex solutions that might be warranted.

Formal problem solving means engaging in a well-organized process of defining the problem you are facing, brainstorming (without screening) possible solutions, evaluating the practicality and probable effectiveness of each solution, choosing one or a combination of these solutions, and following through on your selected solution or combination of solutions.

The following strategy can be used to help you learn the process of problem solving. You should make an effort to practice this method at least a couple of times a week on various problems you might face.

The Problem-Solving Method

Step 1: Identify the Problem

The aim here is to be as specific as possible. Problems described in general, vague, or exaggerated terms are harder to solve and make you feel ineffective when you try to solve them. If you find that your problem description includes "larger than life" issues, you probably need to redefine your problem. To increase the probability of success in solving your problem, you need to define it specifically and accurately.

Example: "I was invited to a friend's pool party and I want to go, but I am embarrassed about getting into my bathing suit and hanging around the pool in it with everyone else."

Step 2: Brainstorm Alternative Solutions

The goal of this step is to brainstorm all the possible solutions to your problem. *Brainstorming means generating ideas without screening or evaluating.* This requires that you think creatively about the various alternatives and also learn to value, appreciate, and uncritically accept your own ideas. The process of brainstorming will result in a comprehensive list of alternative solutions to any problem you face. It will enhance your sense of worth and control as you begin the process of overcoming your habitual, maladaptive strategies for resolving problems.

Example:

1. I could decide not to go.

2. I could go in regular clothes and not swim at all.

3. I could wear my suit under my clothes and see how I feel once I'm there, then make a decision.

4. I could ask the hostess about the guest list and consider how comfortable I would be exposing myself to that crowd, and then make a decision.

Step 3: Evaluate Each Solution

After generating a number of solutions, begin to evaluate each one. At this stage, you should take each item on the list and consider how practical the solution is and how effective it could be. This step is extremely important. Although it is obvious that you would not want to choose a solution that is impractical or unlikely to be helpful, it is sometimes difficult to accurately appraise a potential solution without working through the steps of a formal evaluation. This step helps you fine-tune your search for the solution(s) that will provide the "best fit" and prove the most effective in solving the problem at hand. Evaluate the practicality and effectiveness of each solution, then mark each with a plus of a minus sign:

Example:

"I want to go to the party, so not going to it is not an option." (−)

"I want to have the option of swimming, so having no swim suit with me seems like a cop out." (−)

"It seems better to go with the option of swimming." (+)

"Maybe before I decide I should talk to my friend who is hosting the party." (+)

Step 4: Choose a Solution

The objective here is to choose one or a combination of solutions based on your assessment and your intuition.

Example: "I think I will call the hostess, who is a fairly good friend, and describe my dilemma (i.e., sensitivity about my weight) to her. Then I can feel out the situation before I go to the party—because I do want to socialize. I can be prepared to swim (by bringing my suit or wearing it under my clothes) or choose not to, depending on how it feels when I am there."

Step 5: Follow Through

The objective here is to follow through by implementing the solution(s) you chose.

Example: "OK, I will be going to the party in some type of clothing with my swimsuit under that; there's no turning back now!"

Step 6: Reevaluate the Problem and Review the Problem-Solving Exercise

After implementing the solution, consider the extent to which you succeeded in solving the problem. If necessary, revisit the problem-solving procedure to fine-tune certain aspects of the process if any of the steps have proven to be more difficult than expected (e.g., problem definition, brainstorming).

Example: "This worked well. I was afraid to go but wanted to, and so I figured out a strategy that worked for me by combining a couple of approaches to the problem and some flexible options."

To fine-tune your use of the method, it is essential to practice it regularly, ideally several times a week.

The following worksheet can be used for problem solving. You may photocopy the worksheet from the book or download multiple copies from the Treatments *ThatWork*™ Web site at www.oup.com/us/ttw.

Problem Solving Method Worksheet

Step 1: Identify the Problem

Be specific!

_____
_____
_____

Step 2: Brainstorm all Possible Solutions

1. _____
2. _____
3. _____
4. _____
5. _____
6. _____
7. _____
8. _____
9. _____
10. _____

Step 3: Evaluate the Practicality and Effectiveness of Each Solution

1. _____
2. _____
3. _____
4. _____
5. _____
6. _____
7. _____
8. _____
9. _____
10. _____

Step 4: Choose a Solution

_____

Step 5: Use the Solution

Step 6: Review the Outcome

_____
_____

Modifying Problem Thoughts

In addition to exercises to help you solve certain problems or dilemmas, there are also exercises that can help you keep your thoughts on the right track when you notice yourself slipping into problematic ways of thinking that might either lead to eating problems or other types of distress, such as emotional distress that might lead to overeating or poor self-care in general. For example, a technique called cognitive restructuring can be very helpful when you are troubled by problem thoughts. An example of this would be a situation in which you start to feel self-conscious at a family get-together when you perceive people are watching you to see how much food you are eating because they are concerned about your weight or your eating habits. You start to worry so much about their perceptions of you that you find yourself overeating simply because of the thoughts that keep running through your mind, such as "Everyone is watching me because they think that I have an eating issue." You realize later that although there was nothing to objectively support your perception of your family members' views of you, you made such a strong, internal conclusion based on your "mind reading" of their thoughts that you could not shake these perceptions. You let your conclusions about what others were thinking lead you to a host of problem behaviors (namely, negative feelings toward yourself and others, and overeating). These negative behaviors, thoughts, and feelings could have been avoided if only your thought process had not included so many presumptions about others' thoughts.

This exercise is really quite simple. At the top of the Cognitive-Restructuring Worksheet, you write down the core problem thought with which you have been struggling, then you fill in the two columns of opposing evidence. One column is for objective evidence to support the thought, and the other is for objective evidence to argue against the thought. Once you list all your evidence for each side, you should be able to come to some sort of conclusion that helps you modify the initial problem thought and regain your sense of clarity and calmness regarding the issue that was troubling you.

Figures 13.1 and 13.2 illustrate how this exercise can be used to help you work through your thoughts productively.

Cognitive-Restructuring Method

Step 1: Identify the underlying problem thought.

Step 2: Gather objective evidence or data to support this view.

Step 3: Gather objective evidence to argue against this view.

Step 4: Based on your columns of evidence, come up with a reasoned conclusion that counters the original problem view.

Step 1: Identify the Underlying Problem Thought.

If I eat one piece of pizza, even though it is the only thing being served here, I will lose control and then blow up and gain 5 pounds or more in a day. I can't stop at one or two.

Step 2: Evidence to Support	**Step 3: Evidence to Refute**
I have weighed more in the past on a day after eating pizza.	No single food makes or breaks a healthy eating plan that is designed for weight maintenance.
Pizza does have a lot of calories compared to certain other foods.	I have eaten pizza before and not gained weight.
If I eat one piece, I am afraid that I will end up eating many pieces.	Many of my friends eat pizza all the time and maintain normal weights.
	I haven't really tried eating one piece or a moderate amount of pizza before.

Step 4: Reasoned Conclusion Based on Columns of Evidence

If I eat a moderate amount of pizza, say one or two pieces, it is very unlikely that I will gain a lot of real weight. I just have to set things up so that I stop with one or two pieces and not lose control (by overeating pizza).

Figure 13.1 Example of Completed Cognitive-Restructuring Worksheet

Step 1: Identify the Underlying Problem Thought.

Everyone is watching me because they know I have eating or weight problems and they think I should not be eating so much at this meal.

Step 2: Evidence to Support

I see more glances coming my way from other people.

My daughter said, "Mom, do you really need that?" when I reached for a piece of pie.

When my brother saw me he said, "Wow, it looks like you've gained weight, and I thought you were working on your eating disorder and trying to cut back."

Step 3: Evidence to Refute

It was kind of a free-for-all at the table—everyone was interacting with and looking at everyone.

People always comment on what others are eating; this is just how it is in our family and it might not mean anything in particular when it is done to me.

Some other family members have weight and eating problems, too.

I know I have been watching my eating and my weight and I had deemed this a special meal that I could indulge at a little bit. Given that, I was doing pretty well at this dinner.

Step 4: Reasoned Conclusion Based on Columns of Evidence

People may have been watching me (or maybe not), but it really doesn't matter what they think because I know that I was doing my best with food at this special meal and that it didn't ruin my diet. So the last thing I want to do is overeat because of them. I will make an even firmer commitment to eat healthfully, for myself, for all the right reasons, not for anyone else.

Figure 13.2 Example of Completed Cognitive-Restructuring Worksheet

Step 5: Link this exercise back to your behavior by determining a course of action based on your logical conclusion.

The worksheet on page 85 can be used for challenging and correcting problem thoughts. You may photocopy the worksheet from the book or download multiple copies from the Treatments *ThatWork*™ Web site at www.oup.com/us/ttw.

Challenging Problem Thoughts Worksheet

Step 1: Identify the Underlying Problem Thought

Step 2: Evidence to Support	**Step 3: Evidence to Refute**

Step 4: Reasoned Conclusion Based on Columns of Evidence

Homework

- Continue all aspects of the program (keeping Daily Food Records, working toward a regular pattern of eating, incorporating feared foods into your diet, and engaging in pleasurable alternative activities). Continue also to weigh yourself weekly.

- Practice the problem-solving method (in writing) on at least one occasion this week.

- Use the Cognitive-Restructuring Worksheet to practice the cognitive-restructuring method on at least one occasion to challenge and correct any core problem thoughts you notice.

Chapter 14   *Handling Challenging People*

Goals

- To read and review the entire chapter and discuss with your therapist any questions you might have

- To explore your social relationships by taking note of the number and types of interpersonal situations that have come up in your Daily Food Records and in the other exercises you've completed so far

- To think about making a list of the more (and the less) supportive people in your life (when it comes to your eating disorder)

It is important to be aware of your reactions to the people you are with, the "cast of characters" around you during a given eating situation. The people you eat with can either help or hurt you when it comes to sticking with your program. You have likely already observed that there are helpful people in your life, for example, those who are more like "coaches," and there are less helpful or even harmful people, who are more like "saboteurs." As you work on your eating-related issues, obviously you will want to surround yourself as much as possible with coaches or supportive people, particularly at times of difficulty. Saboteurs are less likely to be supportive and positive and more likely to hinder your progress and be negative.

No matter what, it is helpful to keep in mind your interpersonal or social circumstances at all times, especially if these have had a strong effect on your eating. You might also think about what you will say if others become too "curious" about your eating habits or changes in your eating or exercise habits or about changes in your weight. For example, if someone asks you if you are on a diet when you are simply (and wisely) attempting to avoid a trigger food in a given situation, you might think about a response along the lines of "Oh, I'm just eating to enhance my health!" If you discover that interpersonal problems contribute greatly to your eating-disordered behaviors, spend some time working on these issues by reviewing entries in your food record that address issues with others and any other examples from the problem-solving and cognitive-restructuring exercises from the previous chapter.

Handling Coaches and Saboteurs

You may already have discovered that your relationship with the people you are closest to has begun to change as you have made changes in your relationship to food and other aspects of your eating disorder. Some friends may be envious that you are taking charge of a problem they have not yet addressed themselves. Others may feel "abandoned" in a sense because you no longer enjoy recreational overeating with them. Some might begrudge you this treatment experience because they know you have tried in the past to address your eating problems without success. Regardless, it is important for you to decide how you are going to talk about your commitment to treatment. You can be best prepared by thinking about the people you know and determining who among them are likely to be coaches and who saboteurs.

Write down your plans for dealing with coaches and saboteurs here:

_____
_____
_____
_____
_____
_____
_____
_____
_____

Homework

- Continue all aspects of the program (keeping Daily Food Records, working toward a regular pattern of eating, incorporating feared foods into your diet, and engaging in pleasurable alternative activities). Continue also to weigh yourself weekly.

- Create a plan for dealing with coaches and saboteurs.

Chapter 15   *Preventing Relapse and Maintaining Change*

Goals

- To read and review the entire chapter and discuss with your therapist any questions you might have
- To review the progress you have made in treatment and identify those areas that still need some work
- To consider methods of maintaining your progress
- To create a relapse-prevention plan

Now that you are near the end of your program, it is important to review your progress in order to take note not only of the aspects of your eating-disordered thoughts, feelings, and behaviors that have changed but also of those areas that still warrant improvement. Remember that you can use this book after formal treatment ends to continue to improve your healthy eating habits. In reviewing your progress, if the program has helped you, you will likely first take note of the obvious changes you have made, such as reducing the frequency of your binge eating and/or purging episodes. You will probably also notice an increase in the frequency of regular meals and snacks and in the amount of appropriate, moderate-level exercise you engage in. On the other hand, if you have not been particularly successful in the program, you will probably notice fewer and smaller changes in these same areas.

It is important as you evaluate your experience in this program that you make a concerted effort to identify those aspects of the treatment program that have been most helpful. You might start by thinking about the variety of tools you learned in this workbook. After spending some time thinking through the progress you made and the tools that helped the most, list them on the worksheet provided so that you can have them at your fingertips if you get into some trouble with your eating disorder at a later date. See the example that follows

1. Scheduling regular meals and snacks (while being flexible) and committing to eating not more than six times a day and never skipping breakfast

2. Always keeping food records

3. Weighing in only once a week

4. Using other activities to distract myself when I would have used food in the past—waiting for the urge to eat to go away (it does!)

5. Not using food to distance myself from problems but instead figuring out a way to solve the problems

6. Trying to think more clearly and rationally when it comes to food and my body, and learning and applying strategies to do that

Figure 15.1 Example of Most Helpful Components of Treatment

and use the space provided to list the most helpful tools in your program. Once you have completed this list, make a copy and stash it in a hard-to-forget place for easy access. After you create your list, you might want to create a relapse-prevention and maintenance plan that spells out how you might use your new skills to respond to any eating disorder–related problems you encounter after treatment. We have provided a sample maintenance plan in Figure 15.2.

Most Helpful Components of Treatment:

1. _____

2. _____

3. _____

4. _____

5. _____

Once you identify and list the components of treatment that have been most helpful for you, it is important to recognize and accept the need to continue using these strategies for some time after you've ended therapy. When therapy ends, it might feel tempting to "experiment" with going back to the way things were before treatment,

What worked for me most is the strategy of eating three meals and two or three snacks each day. This regular pattern prevents my getting too hungry—an experience that set me up to binge in the past. Because I am also allowing myself to eat—in appropriate settings and amounts—formerly feared food that I actually crave, these cravings don't get out of control and no longer trigger binges. Although I have always been critical of my body weight and shape, I think the weekly weighing, during this time that I have been experimenting with eating, has helped reassure me that my weight can stay in a stable range even when I am eating nutritiously and regularly. Before treatment, there was no way I would have believed that.

I am worried that at times I still might relapse into a "weight loss" effort of one type or another; for example, it always seems better to weigh 10 lbs less. But I guess I will just try hard to manage my thoughts and emotions when these issues come up, and I will remember to solve my life problems by using strategies that don't involve food because food has never proved to be a helpful, long-term solution anyway.

Figure 15.2 Example of Completed Relapse-Prevention and Maintenance Plan

My Relapse Prevention and Maintenance Plan

"just to see." This could mean starting to skip breakfast again, or resuming your 2-hour-a-day workout sessions, or occasionally allowing yourself to bake cookies at home (a known risk factor for you) and then eating a dozen in one sitting. Likely, this type of experimentation will only lead you back to where you were before treatment; remember, it is the behavior changes that you made during treatment that have facilitated your recovery (to whatever extent that has happened) from your eating disorder. So, it is best if you try as hard as you can to avoid slipping back into your problem behaviors, attitudes, or feelings regarding food and your body.

On the other hand, it can be the case that no matter how hard you try, you experience a setback or lapse, or even a full-blown relapse. What is a lapse? Typically, a lapse is defined as a very brief regression into the symptoms—behavior, attitudes, emotions—that were plaguing you before treatment. For example, a lapse or fairly brief setback might resemble the following: Over the course of a week or maybe two, you twice skip a meal when you know this is not consistent with ongoing recovery from your eating disorder, or on a few occasions you engage in very strenuous exercise sessions of long duration or give in to an urge to purge or to graze all day on snack food. In any case, a lapse or brief setback is a short-term return to the problem behaviors, whereas a relapse suggests a return to the symptoms that lasts up to several weeks or months.

The problem with setbacks is that the longer they continue, the more likely they are to evolve into relapses. Thus, *it is extremely important that you apply the tools that you have known to be helpful as soon as possible after you see a pattern of problem behavior resurfacing.* We cannot overstate the importance of keeping your list of the most helpful components of treatment easily accessible and within reach. If you have benefited from this program, we recommend that you refer to your list, reread this workbook, and push yourself to get back on track as soon as possible if you find yourself slipping. We encourage this type of approach rather than suggesting that you resume any type of treatment, whether CBT therapy or another therapy targeting your eating disorder, because getting yourself back on track reinforces the message that you've learned and mastered all the essential tools. It is these tools, rather than additional "magic" from other sources, therapeutic or otherwise, that will be most useful to you in maintaining your recovery (and over time, continuing to improve).

It is also important to remember that certain vulnerability factors, including sleep deprivation, stress of any kind, alcohol abuse, and the like, can set you up to experience a setback or a relapse. Remember that your eating disorder might always be more "sensitive" and responsive to vulnerabilities, kind of like an Achilles' heel, and for that reason you should always try to stay one step ahead of the problem, closely in touch with your tools, and compassionate about your own process in working through these issues. You should always retain a moderate level of awareness that you are more at risk for eating and body issues than are your friends or significant others who have not struggled with these issues. Be nice to yourself in your continued commitment to recovery. This means committing to getting back on track as soon as possible after a lapse or relapse and *also* understanding that setbacks can happen. Compassion for yourself in your quest for recovery from your eating disorder is essential.

On the other hand, your progress and recovery might be somewhat incomplete. There might be certain areas that still pose problems for you. For example, although your eating behaviors might be mostly good, you might still occasionally fall back on binge eating and purging to alleviate your anxiety about weight gain or to provide a catharsis for other feelings. Or, to a considerable degree, you might still contend with body-image issues that continue to result in not only emotional distress but also restrictive eating behaviors of one type or another that can set you up to binge. These areas of difficulty are as important to note as are the areas of improvement.

Even if you are still struggling with aspects of your eating disorder, the first strategy for you to try is to continue to apply the tools introduced to you here on your own, without the support and aid of a therapist. Give yourself a number of weeks. If after 4 to 6 weeks or so your situation is still unimproved, then it might be important to consider alternative options like full CBT, medication, or a combination of the two. There are also various psychotherapeutic approaches, beyond CBT, that could ultimately help you, including interpersonal psychotherapy (IPT), emotion-regulation therapy, or dialectical behavior therapy (DBT), all of which could be combined with medication. These alternative treatments were discussed in detail in Chapter 4. In any case, give yourself a chance to fully "digest and metabolize" what you've learned from this guided self-help approach to treating your eating disorder before you move on to the next approach. You might be surprised to find out how much you know and can apply on your own, after the treatment sessions end. Many individuals continue to make progress up to a year after treatment with a therapist has ended.

Certain feelings about leaving therapy might arise, despite the encouragement above. These feelings might include relief at the prospect of "graduating" from treatment, sadness or fear at the feeling of being "left alone" with your problem, and loss or feelings of abandonment associated with leaving your therapist. Take these feelings seriously and apply all your tools to address and work through them so they don't become triggers for your eating problems.

We hope this experience in guided self-help therapy for your eating problems will prove useful in other areas of your life. In combination with your own motivation, commitment, and drive, this type of manual and brief therapy sessions can help you meet any challenge in your life.

About the Authors

W. Stewart Agras earned his medical degree from University College, London, England, in 1955 and then completed his residency and fellowship at McGill University, Montreal, Canada. He was an early leader in the field of behavior therapy. At the University of Vermont, he became interested in phobia as a model for psychotherapy research, and, in collaboration with Harold Leitenberg, PhD, discovered that exposure to the feared situation was a principal ingredient of treatment for phobias. After moving to the University of Mississippi Medical Center as chairman of the Department of Psychiatry in 1969, he established the department as an active research center focused on behavioral psychotherapy, establishing the psychology residency program with David Barlow. In 1973, he moved to Stanford University as a professor of psychiatry, establishing one of the first behavioral-medicine programs in the country, and becoming the first and founding president of the Society for Behavioral Medicine. When the upsurge in patients with bulimia nervosa occurred in the late '70s, he began research into the etiology and treatment of the disorder, conducting a number of important treatment trials for bulimia nervosa, together with the first treatment studies for binge-eating disorder. In addition, he has been president of the Association for the Advancement of Behavior Therapy and editor of the *Journal of Applied Behavior Analysis and the Annals of Behavioral Medicine,* and has twice been a fellow at the Center for Advanced Studies in the Behavioral Sciences.

Robin F. Apple received her PhD from the University of California–Los Angeles in 1991 and has published articles and chapters in the area of eating disorders. She has also cowritten a patient manual and a therapist guide that use cognitive-behavioral therapy to help patients prepare for weight-loss surgery. In her current role as associate clinical professor, Department of Psychiatry and Behavioral Sciences, Stanford University, she has an active role training postdoctoral psychology fellows and psychiatry residents to use CBT and other treatment techniques, and has provided short- and long-term individual therapy and group therapy for those dealing with eating disorders and a range of other issues. Dr. Apple also maintains a varied caseload in her private practice in Palo Alto, California, and she is a consultant with the county medical center's eating-disorders program, a contributor to a multi-center weight-loss surgery research study, and has been an expert witness in forensics related to weight-loss surgery.

CPSIA information can be obtained
at www.ICGtesting.com
Printed in the USA
BVHW021233150623
666000BV00013B/335